Praise for *The Perfect Further Education Lesson*

Jackie Rossa has brilliantly crafted a book that succinctly and eloquently addresses the perennial question of deliverers of learning about what constitutes a grade one lesson. Through the use of a wide range of practical examples drawn from the breadth of the FE curriculum, readers can select and adopt key strategies to experiment with within their own delivery sessions.

There is excellent referencing to key components of the Ofsted 2012 Common Inspection Framework (CIF) which deepens the reader's understanding of the essence of this framework in relation to delivering outstanding teaching and learning and allows them to gain a useful insight as to how judgements are made. This knowledge enables the reader to reflect, adapt and adopt working practices which directly enhance their students' learning experience, as well as (incidentally) meeting the CIF observation criteria.

The structure and accessibility of the writing in this book makes it an essential read for every deliverer of learning who is constantly endeavouring to improve their students' learning experience. The clear structuring of chapters enables readers to dip in to topics, or simply to extend or reinforce their existing knowledge. The end of chapter checklists ensure that time-pressed educational professionals can use this book frequently as a useful source of reference.

This book is suitable for those new to the teaching profession and seasoned professionals. The Ofsted CIF is, in itself, an articulation of what constitutes best practice in teaching and learning, and this book definitely delivers on this agenda too.

**Elaine Martin, Director of Quality and Performance,
Vision West Nottinghamshire College**

Jackie Rossa writes with a sound understanding of the challenges and opportunities that staff work with on a daily basis in the FE sector. Her practical ideas are based on sound pedagogical practice and are shared in a simple style that makes this book accessible to all. The explicit use of words such as 'high expectations' and quotes from Toffler will resonate with both staff and managers. Well done and thank you.

**Jane Lord, Learning and Quality Manager,
Blackpool and The Fylde College**

A comprehensive must-read for both practitioners and leaders/managers within the further education sector who wish to provide their students with an outstanding learning experience. This book offers a magical recipe for achieving outstanding teaching and learning and provides a clear interpretation of what is regarded as 'outstanding' under the Common Inspection Framework. This invaluable resource provides readers with a plethora of quick-win strategies and top tips which are essential for busy practitioners, as well as a thorough justification of why the strategies are essential for achieving outstanding teaching, learning and assessment.

The Perfect Further Education Lesson is an inspirational, easy-to-read, practical guide which provides readers with a combination of explanations, resources and top tips. It provides readers with an array of tips for showcasing the progress of learners when the inspector calls, which is the 'hallmark' of an outstanding lesson!

Verity Holman, Teaching, Learning and Assessment Manager

Jackie Rossa puts the common sense back into teaching and learning. This book is essential reading for teachers, but also for managers, observers and others responsible for improving teaching and learning. Not only is it full of helpful tips, but it is so easy to digest that you could do so in a single sitting! I urge teachers to share the content of this book with peers, get to grips with its messages and try out the ideas, adapting and reflecting as they go.

If you need some inspiration to support your teaching and learning practice team meetings, simply use this book. All teachers, no matter how experienced or skilled, will find great value from each and every chapter.

Deborah McVey, Education Consultant, Inspector, Trainer and Head of Improve, Protocol

Jackie Rossa presents her new menu! She has acquired ingredients throughout her career in further education and with private providers. She has worked as a teacher, an advanced practitioner, a coach and a director of quality and effectiveness; currently she is an inspector for Ofsted and a senior consultant for College Leadership services. Her aim is to continue to improve the quality of teaching for the benefit of all learners.

There are many books on the market on how to teach or improve teaching, but this book offers a one-stop set of recipes. It's a new and fresh vision to reassure teachers that what they are doing in the classroom is exactly what their learners need.

The book is user-friendly and easy to navigate with each chapter offering a set of examples and case studies from the FE sector, top tips and ideas, clarifications and quotes as well as references to current trends. The layout, diagrams and illustrations add to the mix and aid understanding.

Throughout the book, the numerous examples and ideas come from a variety of sectors and providers, so whether in construction or arts, in care or maths, foundation learning or horticulture, teachers will relate to them easily. Jackie reminds teachers to use a common-sense approach and be SMART in their everyday practice. She clarifies how to include functional skills, ILT or PLTS in lessons through practical tips and demonstrations.

Employability skills are highlighted throughout as a key focus to prepare all learners for their future working life and how a 'graduate profile' might enthuse learners to think ahead concretely by demonstrating an attitude to learning in the classroom. Questioning techniques, from Socratic questioning to the use of EVS, to support the formative aspects of learning are covered, as is how to track and evidence progress. It pushes teachers to constantly reassess what learners need to do to learn and how they can work collaboratively to achieve their goals. The tick-list at the end of each chapter makes this a very useful tool when preparing a lesson or getting ready for an observation.

On a practical note, I hope the cover of this book is sturdy because it won't stay on a shelf for very long. It will be passed around the office, used in training sessions, transported home to prepare lessons, and maybe even taken on holiday!

Dr Barbara Van der Eecken, Associate Director for Quality, Birmingham Metropolitan College

A great and very refreshing book, written in plain English. *The Perfect Further Education Lesson* provides workable strategies to tackle issues that teachers find difficult such as embedding equality and diversity, and literacy and numeracy, demonstrating progress and developing broader skills. It's not overly theoretical and pedagogical but referenced where appropriate and covers different vocational areas. The case studies bring the book to life and the reader can relate them to their own experiences. It gives teachers the tools to make improvements to their teaching and learning without making huge efforts and so reduces the barriers they put up (time being a favourite).

Written in a user-friendly way with lots of practical ideas to use with students, it echoes much of what I believe makes for outstanding teaching and learning.

Karen Green, Director of Quality Improvement, Chesterfield College

THE PERFECT LESSON

further education

links directly to the Common Inspection Framework (CIF) 2012 criteria for further education and skills providers

Jackie Rossa Edited by Jackie Beere

 Independent Thinking Press

First published by
Independent Thinking Press
Crown Buildings, Bancyfelin, Carmarthen, Wales, SA33 5ND, UK
www.independentthinkingpress.com

Independent Thinking Press is an imprint of Crown House Publishing Ltd.

First published 2014.

British Library Cataloguing-in-Publication Data
A catalogue entry for this book is available
from the British Library.

Print ISBN: 978-178135125-3
Mobi ISBN: 978-178135172-7
ePub ISBN: 978-1781385173-4
ePDF ISBN: 978-178135174-1

Printed and bound in the UK by
Gomer Press, Llandysul, Ceredigion

For Geoff, who made everything possible,
and Nanny, for always believing.

Contents

Acknowledgements

My thanks go to all the learning providers and the hundreds of dedicated, committed teachers who demonstrate brilliant teaching and learning, often in challenging conditions. These teachers have inspired many of the ideas in this book, and I sincerely hope I have done them justice.

Very special thanks go to: Jo Byrne of the East Midlands Centre for Excellence in Teacher Training (emCETT), for her support, encouragement, advice and copious cups of coffee; Jenny Escritt for her support over many years, for always making me stop and think, and for her fabulous illustrations; and Jackie Beere, my editor, who inspired and excited me to write this book in the first place, then enabled me to finally do it.

Foreword

Further education has changed. When I started my teaching career, FE colleges were the places we recommended to our 'awkward' students who wouldn't be able to cope with A levels and who needed a 'fresh start'. They were places where we could go to get cheap but scary makeovers with trainee beauticians. Colleges were invited in to school careers events, hoping that their practical courses would be tempting alternatives for 16-year-old school leavers intent on giving up full-time education to earn some cash.

Fast forward to 2014, and FE colleges offer a full range of vocational and academic courses to degree level. They also take learners from the age of 14, who may be leaving school for a variety of reasons. Now that education is compulsory until 18, so attendance isn't optional, FE teachers and tutors have to be incredibly adaptable and inspiring. Many teachers in FE have a professional or vocational background so they are able to share their experience of the world of work – and how to survive it.

The range of teaching that takes place in FE – from bricklaying to accountancy, animal husbandry, law and sport – presents a unique set of challenges for leaders of these organisations in terms of monitoring the quality of teaching and learning. Many teachers are part time and work on fixed-term contracts. Some have not enjoyed high-quality teacher training and teach with unqualified status. Yet they are subject to the same rigorous scrutiny when the Ofsted inspection team visits, with the focus now clearly on the quality of learning and progress. All teachers need to demonstrate progress and continually improve their classroom practice. The challenge for leadership teams is to support all staff, of whatever background, to deliver the very best lessons that result in the very best outcomes for the students – every day.

Jackie Rossa knows what excellent teaching in FE looks like and delivers it. She is the product of an excellent FE learning experience and knows that the varied opportunities FE presents to students are crucial to their future success.

In this book, she has allied her excellent teaching ideas with her extensive experience of leading and training FE teachers. The book is full of strategies which engage learners and fascinating case studies which demonstrate how well they work in practice. Jackie covers every aspect of being a great teacher in FE and offers so much for you to try and develop in your own style and subject. In addition, she has ensured that all her ideas are well researched and referenced to current Ofsted thinking. In one book, she addresses planning, engagement, assessment, behaviour and student personal development in ways that will appeal to all.

FE colleges are set to play an even more important role in our education system, so her timing couldn't be better.

However, this little book has much to offer any teacher, in an FE or a school setting, because Jackie has gathered together some great ideas that you can adapt and experiment with. At the heart of this book there is an enthusiasm and passion for supporting our young people to learn and grow. And it is contagious ... enjoy!

Jackie Beere, Tiffield

Introduction

The further education and skills sector has considerably less status and fewer resources than schools and universities (Nash et al. 2008), and was memorably described as the 'neglected "middle child"'of the British education system by Sir Andrew Foster (2005: 48). As such, the demands placed on teachers working in this sector are huge, complex and constantly changing.

In recent years, we have seen the introduction of the new Ofsted Common Inspection Framework for Further Education and Skills, study programmes, traineeships, changes to funding, the reform of vocational training and the raising of the participation age, to name but a few. All of this has happened in a climate of economic instability where jobs are hard to get and increasing numbers of young people are classed as NEETs (not in employment, education or training). In addition, the speed of technological, global, social and economic advancement means that the only thing we can be certain of is that things *will* change, and that, first and foremost, we need to equip our learners to thrive in such a world. Learners who now need to stay in education and training until they are 18!

The need for great teaching has never been more challenging or more essential. Teaching and learning are central to the 2012 Common Inspection Framework, and rightly so. It is only teachers who can ensure that learners achieve and succeed, and, if teaching and learning are working well, then everything else (including success rates) will fall into place. This book is designed to go some way towards helping teachers maintain their focus on what really matters, so that they can continue to make that important difference to the lives of so many learners.

Note: This book does not cover the full range of contexts, such as on-the-job training, one-to-one reviews and tutorials. This does not mean that they are not important; it simply means that I could not do them justice here.

The term 'teacher' is used to describe all teaching roles (e.g. trainers, assessors, tutors) and the terms 'learner' and 'student' are used interchangeably.

I have seen every single one of the teaching and learning ideas in this book used to great effect by teachers, trainers and assessors, but that does not necessarily mean that they will work for you. So, take the ones you like and make them your own by changing, mixing, matching or layering – whatever it takes.

Above all, have fun and enjoy your teaching.

Chapter 1
Planning a Brilliant FE Lesson

Brilliant learning rarely happens by accident. It is usually the result of careful planning based on a thorough understanding of your learners. Lesson planning should be an exciting, creative and enjoyable process which ensures that you are well prepared, organised and confident. Good planning also means your learners develop the knowledge and skills that will effectively equip them for life and work.

Before you plan your lesson, however, you need to know exactly what it is that makes learning outstanding in your setting. What are the magic ingredients that will make your lesson brilliant for your learners (and, incidentally, outstanding in the eyes of an observer)? In the same way that you would not expect your learners to successfully complete a task or assignment without knowing what success looks like, you need to know exactly what an outstanding lesson looks like.

The most significant feature of outstanding learning is the progress that learners make. Some of the other essential ingredients that will make your FE lesson outstanding include:

- Learners developing their skills and understanding exceptionally well.
- Demonstrating consistently high expectations for all learners.
- Generating high levels of enthusiasm for participation in and commitment to learning.
- Actively involving and engaging learners in a wide range of activities.
- Fostering resilient, confident and independent learners.
- Learners developing the critical skills needed to achieve qualifications.
- Demonstrating excellent subject and/or industry experience and using this to motivate and engage learners.
- Using assessment as an integral part of the learning process.
- Challenging all learners to exceed their expectations.
- Closely matching support and intervention to individual needs.
- Differentiating tasks and activities for various groups of learners.
- Using collaborative peer learning and assessment.
- Utilising technology to contribute to learner progress and success.

- Making strong links between learning and the world of work.

Teaching outstanding lessons is not easy and every teacher will do it slightly differently. However, the only way you can make sure that you are able to demonstrate the features listed above is to constantly experiment and practice, to take risks and do things differently. To achieve consistently great learning, you need to regularly adapt and tweak your practice. This means that you will probably make mistakes and things will go wrong. But that is the joy of learning, and learning from your mistakes and your achievements will help you to improve.

This may feel difficult at first but, over time, you and your learners will develop the habits of outstanding learning. This means that when the inspector does arrive, they will just see you doing what you usually do – teaching a highly effective lesson.

One factor to bear in mind: planning a brilliant lesson does not mean writing a long, detailed lesson plan. Lesson plans are useful in that they set out what you want your learners to learn and how you intend to achieve this. You need to set clear objectives and assess whether these have been achieved, but keep it smart and simple. Remember also that the lesson needs to deliver progress for all – and that takes planning. As all teachers know, very few lesson plans survive the reality of the learners, so you should regard your plan as a flexible framework for learning, rather than something to be slavishly followed. When it comes to observations, inspectors are looking for well-planned lessons rather than extensive lesson plans – they will make judgements on what they observe rather than what they read.

The rest of this chapter will give you information on how to effectively plan your outstanding lesson, and the remaining chapters will provide you with more detail to explore when you need it.

It is essential to bear in mind that there is no set formula for any lesson or learning. The only thing that really matters is the learning that is taking place and the progress each individual learner is making.

Planning for success

So where do you start when planning your lesson? Many teachers say that they begin with the curriculum content that needs to be covered and the requirements of the awarding body. Whilst this is important, it is all too easy for teachers to get bogged down in it, leading to what Ofsted describes as:

'Lessons [that] do not focus sufficiently on developing learners' skills for employment.'

Ofsted (2012b): 7

Our learners need to develop the skills and knowledge that will enable them to be successful in their future jobs and lives, in addition to those they need to pass the course. Ofsted identifies the broader skills necessary for learner success and career progression as:

'Communication, teamwork, leadership, taking responsibility, reflective thinking, problem solving, independent enquiry and employability.'

Ofsted (2014): 45

The best lessons develop these important skills as well as subject knowledge. Planning your brilliant lessons will become much more straightforward when you focus on what your learners need to do to learn, rather than what you need to do to teach.

Case study

Paul is teaching his group how to prepare a door for painting. Before he starts the lesson, he asks them to identify what a good paint job looks like. He uses the feedback to establish the success criteria for the lesson. Learners are then asked to identify what skills they need to use to successfully paint their door. Paul then asks them which of the skills and processes they feel confident in and where they might need additional help. He uses this as his basis for pairing learners and providing additional demonstrations. At the end of the lesson, the learners review their progress against the success criteria for the finished door and the skills that they have used and developed during the lesson.

It is also important to develop learners' core skills in maths and English:

'Good and outstanding teaching makes the best use of opportunities to create confidence in and correct use of, both English and mathematics, recognising that these core skills are essential to employers.'

Ofsted (2012b): 28

Although this may seem challenging in an already jam-packed curriculum, you should take every possible opportunity to practise, reinforce and develop your learners' literacy and numeracy skills. Using and applying maths and English in a vocational context improves the quality of that learning, making it more relevant and meaningful.

Case study

Lawrie is teaching his class about disease immunity. He gives learners a text on the subject. Each pair skims the text to get an overview and then scans it to identify important information. They then share their findings with another pair and work together to summarise and create questions to ask about the topic. At the end of the activity, they discuss and evaluate not only what they have learned about disease immunity, but also the effectiveness of the strategies that they used to extract information from text.

Top tip

■ Include literacy and/or numeracy opportunities in your planning every lesson.

Planning to develop great learning habits

Good learning habits are important employability and life skills that become habits simply because they are used so frequently that they become second nature. This means that great learning becomes a routine part of your lessons and learners are able to demonstrate these skills without thinking, and talk about their learning in ways that show you have been a very effective teacher, enabling you to consistently demonstrate outstanding learning.

Great learning habits include:

- Arriving on time, being organised and expecting to start work straight away.
- Treating each other and staff with consideration and respect.
- Working hard and expecting tasks to be difficult and challenging.
- Taking responsibility for their own and each others' learning.
- Working independently.
- Seeking feedback on their work.
- Asking good questions.
- Making mistakes and learning from these.
- Evaluating and improving the quality of their work.

'Good and outstanding teaching ... results in young people who not only know the value of being on time, meeting deadlines and managing their career, but also who can deliver the quality of work that employers expect. For young people from disadvantaged backgrounds, these skills can be an escape route from deprivation, and, in some cases, crime and anti-social behaviour.'

Ofsted (2012b): 28

Case study

As Tony's travel learners enter the classroom, they are given 'boarding passes' which tell them where they are sitting and with whom. They immediately begin to work together on their starter task. They each have specific responsibilities within the group, such as leader, checker, scribe and timekeeper. For example, it is the responsibility of the checker to make sure that all learners in the group fully understand what is being learned. At the end of the lesson, Tony asks the learners to evaluate how well they worked within the group, and what they could have done better. The learners give feedback to each other and action plan for the next lesson.

Plan for success by:

- Creating your own 'successful graduate profile' by identifying exactly what skills, knowledge and behaviours your students will need to be successful in their lives and careers.
- Focusing your planning on these skills and explicitly teaching them.
- Developing a skills profile with your learners so that they link this to achieving their goals and aspirations.
- Initiating rituals and routines that become great learning habits.

Planning high expectations and challenge

> 'Staff have consistently high expectations of all learners and demonstrate this in a range of learning environments.'
>
> Ofsted (2014): 54

Having high expectations is probably the single most important thing that you can do for your learners, yet 'insufficient challenge' is one of the most common criticisms levelled at teaching in FE.

It is important to have incredibly high expectations of your learners, and set demanding tasks that are *almost* too difficult for learners to achieve. If students are to make great progress, they need to be out of their comfort zones and working harder than they usually do. This means that they will struggle and make mistakes. But it also means that brilliant learning can take place as they learn from those mistakes. Your job is to make them relish the challenge of working harder and expecting more of themselves. This can be hard because some of your learners may be in the habit of coasting and have never really pushed themselves.

To effectively challenge learners' thinking skills, you should plan to get them all working at the top end of Bloom's taxonomy (i.e. creating and evaluating). In many lessons, teachers simply focus on the lower-order skills, such as remembering and understanding.

Case study

Alayna gives her students a set of questions about a topic they have just completed. The questions are at different levels of Bloom's taxonomy. The learners work in small groups to answer the questions. When they have finished, Alayna asks them to map the questions they have been given to the different levels of the taxonomy. She then asks them to decide which were the hardest questions and why. Finally, they create additional 'hard' questions from the top end of the taxonomy for their peers to answer.

If your course leads to graded outcomes, such as pass, merit and distinction, plan to teach *all* your learners to distinction level. This is not quite as half-baked as it sounds. Distinction-level work requires learners to demonstrate analysis, evaluation, synthesis and creativity. These are not innate talents, but important intellectual skills that can and should be learned by all. These need to be taught explicitly so that learners know exactly what they are.

Case study

Hassan introduces his catering learners to distinction-level criteria by asking them to compare and contrast their mobile phones (analysis), identifying the key features of the different models. He then asks them to decide which phones are best and why (evaluation). Finally, he asks them to create the 'perfect mobile phone', justifying the design features they include, within a price constraint (synthesis/creativity). He gets the learners to link the skills they have just demonstrated to the skills needed to be great chefs and to achieve distinctions in their assignments.

Both Alayna and Hassan are showing their learners what high-order thinking skills look like so they know exactly what is expected of them.

Challenging learners to develop their thinking skills is critical to their success. However, to make sure that teaching and learning 'develop high levels of resilience, confidence and independence in learners when they tackle challenging activities' (Ofsted, 2014: 53), we also need to provide high levels of challenge in other aspects of their learning, such as:

- The development of confidence and interpersonal skills.
- Changing attitudes or beliefs.
- Changes in behaviour.

- The ability to work and learn in different ways and with different people.
- Proficiency in practical skills.
- Learning independently.
- Working to deadlines.

Plan to keep learners engaged and motivated when things get tough by making sure they know exactly what they are expected to do and how to do it. This means that they need to understand the success criteria for the lesson, and that the challenge is difficult but not unattainable. They should also be able to see a pathway that leads to their goal, and that support is available if they need it.

Top tip

- Providing strong and highly visible links to learners' anticipated jobs/careers and future goals and aspirations, beyond the end of course, will enable them to see the relevance of the learning and help to keep them motivated and committed to it. This is particularly important when levels of challenge are high.

Planning to meet the needs of all learners

'Drawing on excellent subject knowledge and/or industry experience, teachers, trainers, assessors and coaches plan astutely and set challenging tasks based on systematic, accurate assessment of learners' prior skills, knowledge and understanding. They use well-judged and often imaginative teaching strategies that, together with sharply focused and timely support and intervention, match individual needs accurately. Consequently, the development of learners' skills and understanding is exceptional.'

Ofsted (2014): 54

Effectively meeting the needs of individual learners means planning to give *all* learners the opportunity to develop the high level of skills and knowledge needed for success. All learners need to be able close the gap between where they are and where they need to be, *regardless of their individual starting points and differences*. This can feel like a mission impossible, yet that is exactly what you need to do for your lesson to be truly outstanding.

Learners in FE arrive with a wide range of skills, knowledge, attitudes and experiences that affect the way that they think and learn. Providing just the right amount of challenge and support so that they all make progress is a tricky balancing act – success will depend on you knowing your learners exceptionally well.

To plan effectively, you need to know where your learners are starting from, their levels of motivation and confidence, and their strengths and gaps in skills and understanding. It is this knowledge that will enable you to effectively demonstrate that you 'match individual needs accurately'.

Some teachers think that meeting individual needs means planning different activities for individual learners. This is not only incredibly time consuming but you also run the risk of making assumptions about learners' potential and reinforcing low expectations.

There are a number of strategies you can deploy that will ensure you provide high levels of challenge and meet the needs of individual learners:

1. Plan to closely monitor the work and progress of learners. This enables you to provide support, focus or encouragement if learners are struggling or off task. It also allows you to ask more of those who finish early or are finding the work easy by setting more demanding targets or deploying them to support their peers.

2. Plan for a significant amount of active, collaborative learning. This is absolutely essential, as learners can only be effectively challenged and supported when they are actually doing something. Most personal, social and employability skills can only be developed when working with others.

3. Plan to ask great open, probing and challenging questions. This enhances the learning of stronger learners whilst providing a ladder of support for other learners to climb (see Chapter 4 for more on this).

4. Plan to use a wide range of current, up-to-date, stimulating, interesting and vocationally relevant resources and examples from industry. All learners need to be able to connect their learning to the reality of the world outside – and video clips, equipment and real-life case studies and scenarios can help this to happen.

5. Plan opportunities for learners to demonstrate their learning in different ways. This enables all learners to access the learning, regardless of their strengths or weaknesses. It often engages them emotionally and can also challenge them to think in different ways. Some ideas include:

   ▪ A Twitter feed or blog.
   ▪ A rap/hip-hop song.
   ▪ A picture/graphic representation (e.g. flow diagram, concept map).
   ▪ A high-priority email message.
   ▪ A radio broadcast.
   ▪ A market stall with ideas for sale.
   ▪ A word cloud in Wordle.

Planning the lesson objectives

Great learning objectives are aspirational, challenging and focused on what the learners will be able to *do* differently at the end of the lesson or workshop. They should have clear links to learners' personal goals, demonstrate your high expectations and include the development of wider personal and employability skills, such as independent thinking and learning. This means that using your assessment unit outcomes won't really do the job!

Whilst it is important that learners see how their learning links to assessment requirements, focusing solely on these can significantly limit opportunities for students to develop the full range of important skills that they will need in their future lives and careers. When evaluating the impact of teaching on outcomes for learners, it is important to take account of the 'learning objectives that are additional to learners' qualification aims.' (Ofsted, 2014: 44).

For your perfect lesson, consider creating just one or two big, overarching objectives that are interesting, open-ended, include behaviours, require high-level reasoning and/or practical skills and have links to real-world applications. For example, 'By the end of this lesson/workshop, you will ...'

- plan how to evaluate and respond safely and effectively to roadside breakdowns in extreme and difficult conditions.
- create comprehensive care plans that will improve the quality of life of people in residential homes.

- present a compelling business case based on sound market analysis that will persuade our 'dragons' to invest in your proposal.
- design and produce a high quality, commercial standard, three-dimensional timber item of your choice.

Making your objectives open-ended and challenging enough to stretch your strongest learners ensures that they are hard wired for differentiation. This is because learners can access them on different levels and in different ways as they require them to use or develop a broad range of generic and specific skills. For example, when producing the timber item above, learners might use advanced woodworking techniques, create unusual or complex designs, produce a particularly good finish and/or demonstrate good organisation and leadership skills. Open-ended objectives allow for choice, flexibility of interpretation and maximise the progress of *all* learners.

Some teachers interpret differentiated objectives to mean having different (and often lower) expectations of those they perceive to be weaker learners, thereby limiting what some learners can achieve. Some teachers differentiate objectives by using All–Most–Some. The problem with this technique, however, is that it can be interpreted as meaning that there is a ceiling on the progress of weaker learners. Other teachers use Must–Should–Could, which shows what progress should look like and makes clear the goals they are working towards. There is always a slight risk that some learners might consider that 'must' is good enough, so make it absolutely clear that everybody is on a journey towards the ultimate 'could'.

Objectives will make the purpose of the lesson clear and provide a benchmark against which you can measure how successful you and your learners have been. These need to be expressed in a language that learners can understand and, crucially, shared with them so that they know what they need to do to be successful. Further ideas for creating brilliant objectives and using success criteria to ensure great progress can be found in Chapter 2.

Creating a climate for learning

Establishing the right atmosphere for learning is essential for a brilliant lesson. The emotional and physical environment will have a significant impact on the way that your learners behave and, therefore, the progress that they will make. How learners feel impacts on their learning far more than what they see, hear and do.

A good climate for learning is one where:

- Learners can trust each other and the teacher to treat them with fairness and respect. Offensive or derogatory comments and put-downs are not tolerated.
- Learners understand that they are a team and that success depends on everybody working together and helping each other to achieve.
- Learners take joint responsibility for their learning.

- Mistakes and errors are a welcome part of learning.
- Boundaries are clear and respected by all.
- Learners expect to work hard and develop good learning habits.
- Learners can clearly see the relevance and importance of what they are learning.
- You believe with a passion that all learners can succeed and, regardless of their starting points, that everybody can change and improve.

Plan to treat your learners as if they are the adult professionals they are aspiring to be. Refer to them as if they are already travel guides, nursery nurses, sports coaches, accountants, chefs, plumbers and so on (e.g. 'As web designers, how should we approach this request?'). This helps to reinforce the relevance of their learning and helps them to see why the skills and behaviour that they are learning are important.

Top tip

- Planning clear links between theory and practical lessons is critical for success. Learners often view these different aspects of their learning in isolation, and we need them to make strong connections between them. Ask theoretical questions during practical activities, and vice versa, to reinforce learning connections. This is particularly important in functional skills or additionality lessons.

The physical learning environment

As far as possible, ensure that the learning environment replicates the industrial environment so that learners get used to working with professional standards and equipment. This makes it easier to demand professional standards of behaviour too.

Case study

On Jo's beauty therapy course, learners have a rota for managing the aesthetics of the salon environment, and monthly meetings are held to discuss any issues or improvement ideas. Learners take responsibility for their own salon space and have to plan for practical sessions by ordering supplies from the dispensary in advance, using their 'virtual' budget. This helps them to understand the importance of planning, requires them to spell technical words and improves their maths skills.

How you organise the learning environment will have an impact on the way that students learn. Arranging tables in groups means that learners can communicate easily with each other and gives you the flexibility to use small group or pair work, as required, without moving furniture.

This type of flexible arrangement is not always practical in workshop spaces, which are often fixed due to health, safety and technical requirements. But don't let that stop you. Put learners in pairs or small groups around workshop stations to enable them to work together if that is what is needed. Always try to bring learners together at the start, end and at key points during the lesson to create a sense of community and collaboration, and to provide structure to the learning.

Using technology

Technology is essential to most students' lives, and can add interest, excitement and engagement to learning. It must, however, earn its place in your perfect lesson by contributing to student progress and learning. Deborah McVey (2013) offers the following useful advice:

> Smart teachers, who use mobile technology well, tend to follow certain steps to ensure success. They ensure the WIFI is easily accessible for all in the class. They have contingency plans such as sharing devices, switching to verbal questions, games or activities if technology fails, and they don't get flustered if it does. Most importantly, they don't use it because it's something they've been told to do and they certainly don't work their lesson around trying to fit mobile technology in. They plan first what learners need to learn, what they need to be able to do, and how best to do that. Where they see that mobile technology can improve the learning, and develop some skills and increase enthusiasm along the way, they use it. In other words, they apply a common sense approach.

Checklist for planning your brilliant lesson

- Have incredibly high expectations of all learners and plan for every individual to make great progress in every lesson. ☑

- Explicitly teach all the core skills and habits that learners need to succeed now and in their future jobs, lives and careers. ☑

- Where possible, plan to include a significant amount of highly active, collaborative and independent learning. ☑

- Engage and excite learners by making strong connections between what they already know, what they are learning and their future jobs, learning and careers. ☑

- Constantly monitor learners' progress so that you can provide support and challenge where necessary. ☑

- Create opportunities to provide rapid, specific and developmental feedback to all learners. ☑

- Create a climate of respect where learners develop great habits and learn through practice, reinforcement and evaluation. ☑

Chapter 2

Engaging Learners from the Beginning

The start of your lesson provides the perfect opportunity to capture the hearts and minds of your learners. Getting them fully and enthusiastically engaged from the very start of your learning session can be challenging, but it is crucial. Those first few minutes set the tone for the rest of the lesson and can make a huge difference to learning and progress.

Get off to a flying start by making sure that students organise themselves and start work as soon as they enter the room. Preparing a meaningful task for them to do as soon as they arrive reduces stress and improves behaviour. It also means that you can quickly accommodate latecomers and sort out any problems without disrupting the learning.

'Raggedy start' activities might include recap quizzes, problems to solve, challenging questions, provocative images or controversial statements to debate. The task should let your learners know that they are in for an exciting time. It must also be:

- Relevant to all learners.
- Interesting, stimulating and challenging.
- Collaborative – learners should have to work with each other.
- Easy to access without instructions or direction from you.
- Short and pacey, but last long enough to cover the time it takes for all learners to arrive.

Of course, not all learners will develop the ability to self-start and work independently without a little help. Good learning habits are developed through repetition and practice, so get them used to working in this way from day one. This is also likely to improve attendance and punctuality, as learners are more likely to get there on time if they know that the lesson is going to start with something interesting and important. Any observer will also be impressed by the way that your learners 'attend, participate in, arrive on time and develop the right attitudes to learning.' (Ofsted, 2014: 44).

As your learners arrive and start work, make sure that you speak to all of them individually. Showing that you care about them and their world by being genuinely interested in what is happening in their jobs, work placements or other interests will engage their emotional brains, making them more receptive to learning. It also means that you can tune in to their moods and feelings, and pick up on any issues or emotions that may impact on their learning.

Making these important connections at the start maximises learning throughout the lesson, so make sure you do this every time, even in your shorter lessons.

Using music to set the scene

Some teachers like to have music playing as their learners arrive to create the right atmosphere for learning. You can choose music that will calm or energise students, or establish a theme that can be referred to and used during the lesson. Turning the music off can be a signal that you want their attention and they should stop what they're doing.

Case study

Marlene's students have responsibility for planning and organising music for their lessons throughout the year.

She gives them the scheme of work and they organise a rota, working in pairs to select tracks to be used as starter or working music. The students are responsible for getting to the class early and setting up the music. Learners have to explain to their peers how the music links to the topic being learned and why they have chosen it. This helps to get the students engaged with the course as a whole as well as individual lessons.

These types of routine can create 'triggers' in learners' brains so that they automatically switch into work mode as soon as they arrive. These habits help learners to settle down, focus and make the transition between what they have been doing and what you need them to be doing in your perfect lesson. Anyone walking into your room will see a warm, productive atmosphere with responsible learners who arrive well prepared and ready to work and learn.

Top tip

- Some teachers cannot access their classroom until the actual start time of the lesson/workshop. If this is the case, rather than making do with an environment that doesn't work for you, make setting up the room an integral part of your starter routine. One teacher uses the end of the lesson to allocate jobs for the next session, such as rearranging furniture, organising the resources and setting up the equipment. This turns a possible problem into a great opportunity to learn about the value of teamwork and collaboration.

Ready for take-off: the starter

So, you are ready and good to go. The students are all present, eager and focused; you are calm, confident and relaxed; and your perfect lesson is about to start. This is the crucial moment when you capture their imaginations, ignite their interest and curiosity, and prepare their brains for the exciting learning to come.

Some teachers use specific starter activities that are separate from the main part of the lesson, whereas others simply have a lively and memorable start to the main lesson. How you do this doesn't really matter, as long as the outcome is learners who are energised, excited and engaged with the lesson. This will also enable you to show an observer how well you generate 'high levels of enthusiasm for participation in, and commitment to, learning' (Ofsted, 2014: 54).

Generally, starters need to be simple tasks with big impact. They should:

- Be short, fast paced, challenging and interesting.
- Have strong links (and preferably a seamless transition) into the rest of the learning session.

31

■ Prepare the learners mentally and physically for learning.
■ Be learner led and collaborative.

Case study

Michelle's learners walk into a very warm classroom. There is a lot of clutter on the tables and the small room is overcrowded with chairs. A radio is playing in the background, the blinds are down, lights are dimmed and the text on the interactive whiteboard is tiny. Michelle begins the lesson despite complaints from the learners. After a few minutes, she stops and asks them why the conditions are a problem. Michelle then uses their responses as a springboard for the objectives for this lesson, which is about effective communication in care settings.

Some ideas for starter activities are listed below. Many of these also serve as raggedy start activities, and can be used at any point during the lesson when you might need to raise energy levels or re-engage learners. Use them to review prior learning, introduce new topics or a mix of both.

Question generator

Tantalise learners with a thought-provoking image, statement, graph or YouTube/video clip, and ask them to come up with a series of questions about it that they want answered. You can make the task entirely open or give them a framework for the questions (e.g. What, Why, When, Who, Where).

Taboo

This works exactly like the word-guessing game and learners usually find it great fun. The students are given a card displaying a word that they have to explain to the rest of their team in less than a minute. They are not allowed to use any of the 'taboo' words also printed on the card. This activity can be used to recap prior learning and to introduce words and concepts to come. This works best when learners work in small teams to compete against each other rather than as a whole group.

Matchmakers

Learners are given two cards. One has a question written on it and the other has the answer to a *different* question. They then have to find the partner questions and answers. This is highly active and generates a lot of debate, particularly if you make some of the questions and answers fairly hard to match.

Hot topic

Learners working in pairs are given a contentious topic to debate along with a position to take on the subject – for example, learners prepare an argument either for or against the statement, 'Should people who have smoking-related illnesses be refused health care until they stop smoking?' This helps students to see different perspectives and develops their listening and negotiation skills. It works really well if students then have to reverse their position, so that they can learn to articulate both sides of the argument.

Pictionary

This generates a lot of energy and enthusiasm, particularly if you introduce an element of competition. Prepare a list of ideas, concepts or objects related to the lesson and put them on separate cards or sticky notes. Divide the class into teams. Team members take it in turn to be the designated artist and draw a selected item within a short timescale, whilst the others try to guess what it is.

Saboteur detective

Learners work in pairs to identify two or three things that would 'sabotage' their safety when working in a practical area – for example, a blocked fire door, saucepan handles not turned in, machine guard off. They team up with another pair who ask questions to work out what the problem is. This is great fun and can really bring a dry topic to life.

Spot the mistake

Learners love this as they enjoy finding mistakes in other people's work, particularly yours! This activity can also help them to understand why common mistakes occur. Ask them to identify the errors in, for example, an essay, recipe, spreadsheet or report. In practical workshops, they can work out what is wrong with your fish dish, mortar joint, risk assessment or wastepipe fitting. To generate interest and challenge, the mistakes should not be immediately obvious.

Case study

Gracie is teaching her holistic therapy learners about essential oils. They gather round a table covered by a huge purple cloth, under which are several indistinguishable objects. The learners work in pairs to take out the objects one at a time, and are encouraged to touch, smell and feel them to work out what they are and how they are related to the topic.

The objects include different parts of plants, tissues infused with oils as well as some obscure items, such as a set of plastic false teeth (myrrh helps heal tooth and gum-related ailments). The learners are totally fascinated by and absorbed in the activity, which generates a significant amount of discussion, questioning, interest and debate about the topic.

Engaging learners with your brilliant objectives

As we saw in Chapter 1, your objectives need to reflect your incredibly high expectations of your learners, plus you need to convince them that they all have the capacity to make great progress during the lesson. Believing with a passion that *all* your students can succeed, and communicating this to them, is likely to lead to increased effort, progress and achievement. However, this is not always going to be easy, especially for those learners who lack motivation or self-belief, but it is essential. The encouraging (or frightening) truth is that we get what we expect. Research tells us that teachers and learners are very good at predicting outcomes, so if both believe that success is possible, it is much more likely to happen.

Whenever you can, display your objectives visually and keep them visible and live during the lesson. One of the problems with PowerPoint slides, for example, is that your objectives disappear from view as soon as you move on, so consider producing a mind map or other visual reminder that you and the learners can refer to as the lesson progresses. If you don't have time to do this before the class, create one *with* the learners as you explain the objectives, adding their thoughts and ideas as you go along (or you could ask learners to create it for you). This can come in handy if an inspector walks in partway through your lesson, as learners can use the mind map to explain where they are and what progress they are making towards the objectives.

Creating success criteria

High expectations and challenging objectives can feel daunting as well as exciting for learners who need to believe that they *can* succeed. Time spent exploring and constructing objectives and success criteria with learners at the start of the lesson can pay dividends in terms of levels of engagement and exceptional progress later on. This is because learners are able to take personal ownership and responsibility for achieving them.

Top tip

■ Don't get hung up on terminology. It doesn't matter to your learners if you use the term objectives, outcomes, goals, learning intentions, success criteria and so on. What matters is that learners have some idea of what they are supposed to be learning and why. Inspectors also only care about the impact of what you do, not about what you call it.

If objectives help learners to see what they are going to learn, and why they are going to learn it, success criteria help them to see exactly what the destination looks like and what they need to be able to do to get there. For example:

Objective: Present a compelling business case based on sound market analysis that will persuade our 'dragons' to invest in your proposal.

Activity: Work in teams for the rest of this lesson to prepare the business case.

We will be successful if we:

■ Persuade the dragons to invest in our proposal for the amount we ask.

■ Make a good business case for our plan.

■ Analyse the data, including future markets, effectively.

To be successful we need to:

- Find out where to get hold of the data we need.
- Search the internet to find out what similar companies are doing.
- Decide which data sets will be most useful for us.
- Analyse the data available on current markets and find out what the trends are.
- Allocate team jobs so we don't waste time.
- Work out how we can summarise the benefits of our proposal.

Success criteria are most effective when they show learning as a journey. This enables all learners to see where they are and what they need to do to make progress. This promotes differentiation by providing a route map for even the weakest learners to achieve success, and is a great way of demonstrating to an observer how effectively you are meeting individual needs.

Engaging learners in developing objectives and success criteria

If learners are to achieve success, and make progress, they need to have a clear understanding of what the lesson objectives and success criteria *really* mean. As we've seen, they need to know what they are going to learn, what success looks like when they get there and, crucially, *why* they are learning it in the first place. Learners can only achieve this level of understanding if they work it out for themselves.

Engaging students with objectives is all about letting them in on the 'learning game'. They need to see right from the start how success in this lesson will make a difference to them personally and help them to achieve their bigger goal of becoming a top chef, great coach, brilliant builder, amazing accountant, software genius and so on. You will need to convince your students that the journey they are about to embark on is exciting, relevant and useful to them.

This can be tricky when teaching certain topics – for example, legislation or health and safety – and there will be times when you will need to generate your own passion and enthusiasm for the subject in order to communicate it successfully to them. This is well worth doing: your excitement about the subject will impact on your students, increasing their curiosity and motivation as they try to work out what is so fascinating about it.

Case study

Al is teaching his learners about food poisoning. To capture their interest, he has billed the topic as: 'Monster Invasion 2: The Battle for the Body', and invites them to become a taskforce whose job it is to save the body from this peril!

One great way of helping learners to see the relevance of learning is to get them to find it for themselves by using the connective 'So that ,,,' For example:

> *Teacher*: Today we are learning how to analyse screening forms – why?

> *Learners*: (*Learners discuss options*) So that we can be more confident when making decisions about products to use and give our clients great advice. [Not that they would say it quite like that!]

Case study

Lucy asks her learners to turn the lesson objectives into a mind map and write their individual goals against each of the objectives. They then update and review these as the lesson progresses.

The benefits of engaging learners with objectives and success criteria at the start of the lesson are massive:

- Students' confidence and motivation improve because it enables them to see that success *is* possible, and shows them the skills they need to use or develop to achieve them.

- The more learners understand what is expected of them, the more they will be able to take additional responsibility for monitoring and directing their own learning. Students should be encouraged to develop independent learning skills.

- ▨ Self and peer assessment activities are more meaningful and successful because learners have a vocabulary to discuss their learning and talk about how they can improve.
- ▨ Any mismatch between what you think is a good outcome for the lesson, and what they might consider a good outcome, get sorted out right at the start.
- ▨ Relationships improve – a sense of 'in it togetherness' is generated as you all work towards the same goals.

When students take part in developing criteria, they are much more likely to understand what is expected of them, 'buy in' to the learning and make great progress. What follows are some ideas for engaging students with objectives and success criteria.

Question time

This is simple, but effective, and requires learners to use reasoning skills and to activate prior learning. Students work in small groups or pairs to create questions about the topic that they should be able to answer by the end of the lesson. They pick the most important questions to share with the whole group and read them out. You can then ask them to evaluate which ones will be harder to answer than others. These questions can then be used during and at the end of the lesson to evaluate progress.

Breaking news!

Learners create a headline that summarises what they will have learned by the end of the lesson. This could be in the form of a newspaper headline, Facebook status or tweet. They can do this before or after you reveal the learning objectives, depending on what you want to achieve. Some teachers like to do this before and then get the students to revise it after they have shared the objectives.

Skills scan

This is a great way of helping learners to see what they need to be able to do to achieve the lesson objectives. Learners are given a set of 'skills cards'. These contain personal, social and employability skills (including English and maths) as well as subject-specific and intellectual skills. Here is a set of generic skills that one teacher used in a recent lesson:

Analysis	Leadership	Remembering information
Application	Listening	Report writing
Coaching	Literacy	Researching
Communication	Maths (numeracy)	Resilience
Concentrating	Motivating others	Self-awareness

Conflict resolution	Negotiating	Supporting others
Creativity	Organisation	Teamwork
Debate	Persistence	Working independently
Decision making	Persuading and influencing	Working to deadlines
Empathy	Planning	
Encouragement	Prioritising	
Evaluation	Problem solving	
ICT	Reflecting	

Learners used the cards to create a most/least important skills continuum for that lesson. This reinforced the importance of skills development, and helped the learners to recognise the range of skills they would need to achieve success. This can be taken a step further by asking learners to identify which skills they feel most/least confident about.

Change questions

You do not need to create complicated tasks to engage learners in objectives. You could ask some simple yet powerful questions, such as:

■ What will be different if we meet this objective?

■ What questions do you want to ask about this objective?

■ How will we know we have met this objective?

■ What do we need to know and do to meet this objective?

Surprise, surprise

There may be times when you really do not want to share the objectives at the start of the lesson – perhaps it will limit the potential of the learning activities or spoil the impact of unexpected outcomes. This is absolutely fine as long as your reasoning is sound, you do actually have an objective and progress towards it is evaluated at some point during the lesson.

Here is an example of how one teacher went about this with their group of public service students.

Case study

Sharon wanted her group to evaluate the impact of the media on public services and consider how this might affect them in their chosen career. She particularly wanted them to understand the emotional impact of media coverage, and to experience it for themselves.

■ Each group of learners had a set of pictures, videos and clippings from recent news stories. The groups had the same topics but the information was presented in different ways – some factual and others emotive and 'sensational'.

- Learners discussed how the material affected their feelings about the people and scenarios described.

- The groups shared their responses to the news items, quickly realising that they had significantly different responses to the same topic.

- Students then discussed and explained what they had learned from the activity, how this might affect them in their future jobs, what they thought the session objectives were and what they wanted to know more about.

Sharon then asked her students what the purpose of the activity was. Students said:

- So we realise that we all have different ways of looking at the same thing and there is sometimes not a right or a wrong way.

- So we know that seeing pictures or reading a news story can make you feel really upset or angry about something, even if it isn't all true.

- To make us see how important media coverage is to the way that people see public services. They pay for them, so they expect certain standards.

- To see the difference between objective and subjective, and that subjective is probably less accurate but more interesting to people and sells better.

When asked how this would impact on them in the future, the learners said:

- It has made me realise that I've got to be so careful about what I say and do as a police officer – somebody could twist what I say to mean something else.
- I know that people will look at you differently depending on which stories they read or believe.
- What people think about you can affect the money you get from the government and change the way you have to do your job, so you need to be really careful about who you talk to.

Many learners said that they understood more about how different groups are represented (or misrepresented) in the media, and how this can lead to skewed perceptions about people on the basis of, for instance, gender or ethnicity. This was a great way of ensuring that 'equality and diversity are integrated fully into the learning experience' (Ofsted, 2014: 55).

Checklist for engaging learners from the beginning

■ Have incredibly high expectations of yourself and your learners, and communicate these along with enthusiasm, passion and a genuine belief that they can all succeed. ☑

■ Establish secure routines, habits and rituals that help learners to feel secure and minimise stress and disruption. ☑

■ Make sure that learners have something challenging, interesting and meaningful to do from the minute they enter the room, and that they know they are expected to start work straight away. Don't waste a second of learning time with administrative tasks. ☑

■ Hook them into the start of the lesson by using powerful, unusual, provocative and emotionally compelling resources and activities. Fire their imaginations and stimulate interest and curiosity. ☑

■ Set objectives that make it clear to learners exactly what they are learning and why they are learning it. Make sure the objectives are aspirational, open-ended enough to allow for differentiation and include the development of personal, social and employability skills. ☑

■ Involve learners in co-creating objectives and success criteria so that they have a clear picture of what excellent progress looks like and how to achieve it.

These were all powerful outcomes, and if Sharon had selected one or two of these at the start of the lesson, it is possible that some of this deeper learning might not have taken place.

Chapter 3
Behaviour for Learning

'A positive, caring, respectful climate in the classroom is a prior condition to learning.'

Hattie (2012): 70

Developing great habits that lead to effective behaviour for learning takes time, determination and practice, but the rewards are well worth it. When your students become resilient and confident self-managers, who can work independently and take responsibility for their own learning, their chances of rewarding and successful lives increase hugely. Your perfect lesson will also be judged outstanding. Behaviour for learning helps you to demonstrate 'the impact that teaching has in promoting the learners' spiritual, moral, social and cultural development' (Ofsted, 2014: 54).

Engaging learners in exciting and challenging tasks that are relevant to their goals and ambitions is the best way to ensure positive behaviour, but it does not guarantee it.

You will also need to be ruthlessly single minded about establishing a climate of mutual care, trust and respect where behaviour which disrupts learning is not tolerated. This is crucial. Poor behaviour stops students learning and has absolutely no place in your perfect lesson.

Excellence is not an art, but a habit.

Aristotle

Developing a climate for learning

Strong and effective working relationships make a significant difference to the way students learn and behave. Do this by treating every single learner with respect and consideration. Do this relentlessly, every single day and in every single lesson, and expect them to do the same with you and each other. This will soon become a habit that will extend into their lives and relationships outside college too. The secret is relentless consistency.

No matter how much you try, there will sometimes be students (or even whole groups) that you don't like or find difficult to teach. This is when you need to grit your teeth and treat them as if you genuinely like them and expect them to behave. Learners usually live up to expectations (positive and negative) and eventually their behaviour *will* start to improve. You will also find it less stressful to behave in this way, and may soon find that you do actually like them – warts and all!

Top tip

- The establishment of a positive culture in your learning sessions is entirely down to you, as students will mirror your behaviour, values and attitudes. Be unremittingly kind, considerate and, above all, consistently fair. Show them that you care deeply about their learning by believing with a passion that they can all succeed and never, ever giving up on them.

You should have zero tolerance for put-downs, mockery and offensive or derogatory comments. Be rigorously consistent about this and expect the same from your students. These behaviours undermine learning by discouraging participation and can damage confidence and self-esteem. They may also be symptomatic of bullying. Don't be fooled if learners on the receiving end seem amused – joining in can be a way of protecting themselves. Once students understand that this behaviour is unacceptable, it becomes easier to manage – a sharp reminder will usually do the trick. Make sure you balance this with genuine praise and encouragement when learners support each other with constructive and encouraging comments.

> 'Mutual respect amongst learners, reflecting the approaches and attitudes of staff, reduces the potential for bullying and harassment.'
>
> Ofsted (2013a): 4

Create a team ethos in all lessons where:

- Learners understand that you are 'in it together' and take collective responsibility for each others' learning.
- You have frequent, frank and honest discussions about what is and isn't working, and resolve problems that affect learning together.
- Peer support is a component of all lessons and students know that they *all* make better progress when they support each other to achieve.

Always be genuine and 'real' with your learners. Show them that you too are fallible by openly admitting your mistakes and apologising when necessary. Acknowledging that you cannot possibly know everything is incredibly liberating – and gives you permission to shamelessly exploit the skills, knowledge and experiences of students in your lessons! This enriches the learning for everybody, boosts confidence and self-esteem and helps students to see the importance of their own contribution to learning.

Learning rules!

For behaviour for learning to be effective, students need to be absolutely clear about what their roles and responsibilities are, what is and is not acceptable, and what will happen if they cross the line.

Learning rules are most effective when they are developed with students, as peer power usually guarantees enforcement. Consider creating a charter with the students that clearly sets out 'how we do things around here'. This helps learners to understand what is expected of them and makes them jointly accountable for upholding the team 'rules'. It is essential that all rules are designed to enhance learning and that students are absolutely sure *why* they are important.

Top tip

- Consider making your behaviour for learning charter reciprocal – work with the students to decide what behaviours they need to see from you in return. This is incredibly empowering for you and the students, and strengthens the team ethos by making you an integral part of it.

Learning rules should be:

- Inclusive – they apply to everybody.
- Learning focused – it is clear how they will help learning.

- Linked to consequences – learners need know what will happen if rules are broken.
- Positive – rules should, as far as possible, describe positive expectations rather than negative behaviour (e.g. 'listen to each other' is better than 'don't talk over each other').
- Written as behaviours – this clarifies what should and should not be done.

Here are a set of learning rules created by a group of Level 2 engineering students (with some prompting from the teacher):

- Listen to each other properly and learn from each other.
- Help each other out if we get stuck.
- Look out for each other all the time.
- Treat each other with respect – like we want to be treated ourselves.
- Apologise if we mess up and do or say things we shouldn't.
- Work hard and do our best – always, even if we are fed up or tired.
- To say when we don't understand and ask for help if we need it.
- Learn from mistakes – our own and others'.
- Respect the opinions and beliefs of others even if we don't agree with or like them.
- Make sure we always work safely in the workshop and help each other to work safely.

■ Phones on silent and only use them when we get permission. Never use them in the workshop.

Once your rules have been agreed, reinforce them as often as possible through feedback and dialogue. Get the students to create a poster or wall chart so that they can be referred to constantly, and take it with you if you move rooms. Tap into the power of peer pressure by getting them to challenge each other if they transgress – they are their rules, after all!

There will, of course, be a host of other rules that are non-negotiable, and it is essential that students are fully aware of what these are and understand why they are important to their learning. Learners are much more likely to follow rules when they can see their purpose. Understanding the importance of formal and informal rules is an essential employability skill, as learners will encounter both wherever they work.

Students will obviously test the rules at some point. If they do behave badly, deal with the behaviour firmly, fairly and follow through with any sanctions. It is essential to do this consistently and rigorously. Students feel a profound sense of injustice when teachers do not manage the behaviour of unruly students, particularly when this makes it harder for them to learn.

Top tip

■ When a student misbehaves, deal with the problem and *then put it behind you.* Never hold a grudge against an individual. Start each day, lesson and activity with the same high expectations of their behaviour and learning as you did before the incident. This teaches them what real respect looks like, shows them that you value them as a person and can help change their future behaviour patterns.

The X-ray factor

It is well worth cultivating the skill of 'withitness' (Kounin, 1977). Withitness is what makes students think you have x-ray vision or eyes in the back of your head – and can earn you huge amounts of credibility and respect. It projects your presence into every corner of the room and signals loud and clear that you are acutely aware of everything that is going on. Even when you are having a conversation with one learner, your withitness radar is scanning the room for signs of disengagement, boredom, confusion, low-level chat or disruption which, when detected, you nip firmly in the bud. (This is just as important with groups of adult learners where signs of disengagement may be more subtle.) This sort of vigilance prevents misbehaviour before it starts and enables you to maintain momentum by responding quickly if interest levels start to wane. Make sure that you notice and respond to particularly good work and behaviour too.

Top tip

> ▨ Wherever possible, reinforce effective learning behaviour by 'catching' learners doing something right and praising it so that everybody can hear. This reminds students what effective learning behaviour looks like and shows those students who may be seeking attention that the best way to get it is to demonstrate good behaviour!

Laters!

Punctuality is an important employability skill, so Ofsted expect learners to 'arrive on time and develop the right attitudes to learning' (Ofsted, 2014: 44).

Good timekeeping demonstrates integrity, respect for others and a commitment to learning, whereas lateness often disrupts it. Not all lateness can be avoided but you will need to deal with it effectively without disrupting the rest of the class. Here is how some teachers manage it:

Top tips

> ▨ When Natalie's business learners are late for her class, they are required to put their identity badges in a box

at the front of the room. When they collect their badges at the end of the lesson, Natalie discusses their lateness with them and, if necessary, sets targets or applies sanctions. In this way, the class is not disrupted by lateness, but everybody knows it is going to be dealt with and challenged.

- Jan's students knock on the door and wait if they are late. At an appropriate point, Jan opens the door, has a quick chat with them about why they are late and settles them into the class.

- Yvonne leaves one or two empty chairs near the door to minimise disruption by late arrivals, who then sit there until she is able to talk with them about being late.

- Some teachers have a policy of marking a student as absent on the register until they explain their lateness at the end of the lesson. If the explanation is accepted, the mark is converted to a 'late'.

Judge lateness carefully and fairly. Sometimes there will be a genuine reason that could not be helped, so you will need to listen to what learners have to say. But you must also make it clear to the student involved, and the rest of the group (and any observer), that lateness will be addressed at some point, even if you cannot deal with it there and then.

There will be times (particularly with adult learners and those with caring responsibilities) when persistent, unavoidable lateness will need to be carefully negotiated and managed. In the interests of fairness, make sure that learners in this situation know what their responsibilities are in terms of catching up with minimum disruption to the rest of the group.

Things to avoid

Avoid Asking learners why they are late in front of the class. The answer may be personal or embarrassing, and you run the risk of confrontation if they refuse to tell you.

Avoid Lock out. Refusing students entry to a class if they are late is fairly common practice in some departments, but it sends a message that learning is not a priority. You also risk long-term retention issues as learners who get behind are more likely to miss future lessons and eventually leave the course.

Avoid Flexitime! If a learner is not considered late until, say, five minutes have passed, that then becomes the new start time. Late is one second past the start time. Always.

The use of mobile phones is often a source of tension between students and teachers – having hard and fast rules about their use is increasingly difficult. Many teachers capitalise on the learning potential of phones and students often make good use of them in lessons to blog, vote, ask and answer questions, make notes, take photographs or videos and so on.

Furthermore, a growing number of learners have care responsibilities and need to be contactable in an emergency. The responsible use of mobile phones is an important employability skill so, unless your policies forbid it, let students bring their phones into lessons and teach them how to use them responsibly – for example, 'It's okay to use the internet when you're doing some research, but not when you should be listening to others.'

Learning to learn

'Since we cannot know what knowledge will be most needed in the future, it is senseless to try to teach it in advance. Instead, we should try to turn out people who love learning so much and learn so well that they will be able to learn whatever needs to be learned.'

Holt (1964): 37

In today's fast-changing and information rich world, it is increasingly important that students develop the transferable skills and competencies that will help them to be successful in the workplaces of the future. Learning to learn is the most important skill of all: students need to know how to learn, how to keep on learning and how to make good use of what they know throughout their lives.

Most social, emotional and behavioural skills can be learned. You need to decide exactly what habits, dispositions and attitudes your learners need, so that these can be explicitly developed. The Qualifications and Curriculum Authority worked with employers to develop a useful list of personal, learning and thinking skills (PTLS) that have been used to underpin qualifications.

The six main areas of skill are:

1. Independent enquirers
2. Team workers
3. Creative thinkers
4. Self-managers
5. Reflective learners
6. Effective participators

These abilities have been billed as essential for helping young people to become successful learners, although they are just as applicable to adult learners.

> 'Personal skills are those which give young people the ability to manage themselves and to develop effective social and working relationships. Thinking and learning skills mean knowing how to learn independently and adapt to a range of circumstances. Together these skills are essential for raising standards, further learning, employment and dealing with a range of real-world problems.'
>
> DfES (2005): 41

Where the PLTS are used and implemented well, teachers use them as a basis for working with learners to personalise the skills and make them their own, thereby ensuring that students see how important they are to learning. It is well worth enlisting the help of your learners in creating their own 'critical skills' list.

Case study

During induction, Anna and her accountancy students created an 'outstanding learner' profile by identifying the behaviours that they considered important for their lives and future careers, as well as successful completion of the course.

They agreed that outstanding accountancy learners:

- Work well independently.
- Are resilient, persistent and determined.
- Are highly motivated and enterprising.
- Work well with others and as part of a team.
- Take responsibility for managing their own learning and behaviour.
- Communicate well and treat everybody with respect.
- Help and support each other.

The group spent some time clarifying each of the behaviours and giving examples of when they might demonstrate them. Anna and her learners used this profile throughout the year as a framework for setting individual and group targets, and reviewing their learning and progress. This strategy worked exceptionally well, mainly because it was devised by learners and teachers working together. Ensuring learners understand what we mean when we talk about, for example, resilience or motivation, makes these skills much more accessible and gives the students a vocabulary to talk about learning.

Case study

Bailey teaches English for speakers of other languages (ESOL), and asked his learners to agree a 'respect contract' that set out how they would treat each other. This is what they came up with.

We:

- Listen to each other when speaking and don't finish others' words or sentences.
- Never laugh or make fun when someone goes wrong.

> ■ Are patient with each other because we are trying hard to learn.
>
> ■ Help each other learn and look after each other.
>
> ■ Treat each other the same, even if we don't agree with their culture or opinions.

Embed the development of learning to learn skills throughout your teaching by:

■ Setting high expectations for students' social, personal and emotional behaviour.

■ Setting achievable, individual targets.

■ Giving feedback that recognises and rewards behaviour that maximises learning.

■ Engaging learners in stimulating activities that explicitly use and develop these skills. This is crucial: if learners are to develop and demonstrate resilience in the face of failure and frustration, they will need to experience it! Build opportunities for these experiences into all lessons and activities, and make sure that learners get feedback on how well they are developing and making progress with them.

■ Help learners to see that failure and mistakes are welcome, natural and essential to learning, and model every mistake as a learning experience. This helps students to embrace challenge and take risks. Help them to feel safe enough to do this by explaining why failing is important and teaching them how to cope when they get it wrong.

Case study

Lisa is teaching her functional skills learners about ratio and percentages, a topic they are finding hard. Many are also anxious, having struggled with this at school. At the start of the lesson she reassures them by saying: 'I know this is going to be difficult, but we will stop every ten minutes or so and find out how it is going. We will help each other out if any of us get stuck or don't understand. It will be interesting to see which bits are easy and which are hard, as it will tell us how our minds are working. I will show you what you need to do to learn this well, and I know we can do it if we all work together.'

We convince learners by what we do rather than by what we say, so you need to show by your responses that you genuinely value learning from failure and mistakes. Create plenty of opportunities for learners to make mistakes, and then openly explore and discuss them, highlighting the positive learning that emerges. This gives learners confidence that it really is okay to get it wrong and that they will be always treated fairly and with respect when they do so.

One skill well worth developing is that of a 'growth mindset'. The concept of a growth mindset was first outlined by Carol Dweck (2006), who found in her extensive research that people with a fixed mindset attribute success to innate ability – for example, talent, genetics and luck – and tend to be less successful than those with a growth mindset. Individuals with a growth mindset assume that mastery comes from effort and time spent learning and developing through making mistakes and responding to feedback. Employers place a high value on staff who can demonstrate this type of thinking, which means that helping our learners to develop a growth mindset is one of the most valuable things that we can do for them.

> 'What is the point of having an individual with the complete skills if they haven't got the mindset in which to use them? Someone with the right mindset will be more than willing to learn and develop the skills required, giving you the perfect candidate.'
>
> Melissa Mezzone of Geopost UK,
> quoted in Reed and Stoltz (2011): 42

Here are some ideas for teaching a growth mindset:

- Remind learners constantly that mistakes and failure are an important part of learning, and that it is what we do in response to these mistakes that is significant.
- Praise the effort, time and commitment that learners put into a task rather than their ability or a successful outcome. This helps them to see what the key to success really is.
- Give feedback that tells learners specifically what they have done well and why it was good (learners often attribute their success to luck or something else outside their control).
- Set very high standards for all. Do not accept learners simply 'doing their best'. This means they are working within their comfort zone and we want them out of it, making mistakes and discovering what their potential really could be.

■ When students don't know how to do something, or get it wrong, tell them the truth and help them to work out how to improve.

■ Teach them that it is natural to feel insecure and vulnerable whilst learning.

Case study

Jon wants his learners to develop a growth mindset. He explains to them what the difference is between a fixed and a growth mindset, and then asks them to answer the following questions:

■ What happens when learning gets hard? What do you usually do and say?

■ If you are using a growth mindset, what might you say to yourself? To each other?

■ What could you try if you get stuck?

■ What should I say to help you?

Your perfect lesson should always include time for learners to develop the skills of reflection and metacognition (thinking about learning) through discussion with each other. Reflection helps students to make sense of their experiences and become conscious of *how* they are learning so that they can plan routes for future action. These are arguably the most important skills to develop, and also the hardest, so make sure that students get plenty of time to use and practise them.

Virtual learning

Technology is central to the lives of most young people – they are often skilled in using it and are frequently more motivated and engaged when they do so. There is an increased expectation that students will continue to learn outside of learning sessions and, in particular, make good use of any available technology, such as virtual learning environments (VLEs).

Whilst many learners might be technically competent, not all of them have the skills that are needed for effective independent learning. These important skills need to be explicitly taught and learners should be provided with opportunities to practise and improve them, if they are to make the most of new technologies.

Creating independent learners

Students need to know precisely what independent learning skills are if they are to develop them. Jackie Beere (2010: 75) has identified that good independent enquirers can:

■ Identify clearly the questions and answers to sort out.
■ Plan and carry out research and understand how choices affect outcomes.

- Explore issues and events or problems from different points of view.
- Analyse information and judge how important it is.
- Understand how decisions and events can be affected by the situation, people's beliefs and feelings.
- Back up their conclusions using thoughtful arguments and reasoning.

Teach learners the skills of independent learning by building them up gradually and increasingly transferring responsibility for learning over to them, thereby helping them to see where they use these skills in workshops, lessons and other areas of their life.

Case study

Zak wanted his students to begin to develop their independent learning skills. He gave his learners a task that asked them to:

- Individually conduct an internet search.
- Post their findings, along with a short evaluative summary, onto the VLE by a given date.
- Participate in an online forum and make a minimum number of posts that comment on other students' findings.

■ Discuss and evaluate their experiences at the next class meeting.

Zak made sure that each episode of independent and virtual learning was followed by a face-to-face discussion during which learners could share their successes and frustrations. These meetings are essential as they hold learners accountable for their contributions and increase levels of engagement and participation.

Over time, Zak increased the complexity of the independent learning tasks whilst reducing the amount of direction and support. In this way, his learners became increasingly skilled at working independently.

Create independent learning experiences in lessons where learners have to find out information for themselves, and then present, explain and teach it to each other. This not only creates longer lasting learning, which learners are more likely to remember, but also develops emotional and learning to learn skills as students begin to see the value of supporting each other to achieve.

Checklist for behaviour for learning

- Develop and maintain strong and effective relationships by consistently treating every student with unconditional trust, care and respect in every situation. Know that confidence is catching – if you genuinely believe in them and encourage them to do their best, they will succeed. ☑

- Create a climate where students feel safe and emotionally secure to learn, by being scrupulously and consistently fair at all times and refusing to tolerate any behaviour that disrupts learning. Instil confidence and courage by treating failure, errors and mistakes as wonderful learning opportunities and help students to see why they are crucial to learning. ☑

- Work with learners to establish clear rules and boundaries that help them to feel respected and ready to learn. Maintain these rigorously and deal with any transgressions firmly, fairly and positively. ☑

- Develop and embed a team ethos where learners care about each other and support each other unconditionally to learn and achieve. They should understand that, in doing so, they are also accelerating their own progress. ☑

■ Explicitly teach, develop and reinforce social, emotional and learning-to-learn skills. Help students to understand why they are important and consistently model them yourself. ✓

■ Engage learners in exciting, challenging and collaborative learning activities that sustain their interest and motivation. Get feedback from them constantly on how well the learning is going and use this to adjust and adapt your teaching. ✓

■ Share what you are doing with other teachers and enlist their support and cooperation to embed and reinforce effective behaviour for learning in all learning sessions. ✓

Chapter 4

Ensuring They Make Progress Every Lesson

Progress is, without doubt, the hallmark of an outstanding lesson. This means that you need to ensure that *all* your learners 'consistently make very good and sustained progress in learning sessions' (Ofsted, 2014: 54), particularly those that need it the most. Inspectors will make their judgements about the effectiveness of your teaching based on the extent and quality of the progress that learners make.

Exceptional progress means that learners are able to demonstrate significant improvements in their skills and knowledge. This includes personal, social and employability skills as well as subject- and/or industry-specific skills and knowledge. They should also be 'self-assured, confident and courteous and well prepared for their lives beyond college' (Ofsted, 2013a: 1).

Whilst it is true that demonstrating individual learner progress in all lessons can feel tricky, it is absolutely essential. Effective teaching, learning and assessment *must* result in learners making progress. The challenge, therefore, is for you to create the climate and conditions for great progress to take place, and to ensure that the extent of that progress is clearly visible to you, your learners and, of course, to an inspector.

Top tips

- Prepare for an inspection by having all your learner profiles, along with any resources or needs identified, ready for observers to scrutinise. Decide where you want the inspector to sit – ideally where they can get the best possible view of your brilliant lesson. This will help you to feel more confident and in control.

- It is worth explaining to your learners what is going to happen and why, and that inspectors may want to talk to them and look at their work. Learners usually support their teachers very well during observations.

Mind the gap!

Learners are most likely to make brilliant progress if they can see for themselves the gap between where they are starting from and where they need to get to *in the lesson*. They need to be absolutely clear about objectives and success criteria so that they know what great progress in this lesson looks like, and where they currently are in relation to it. They are more likely to take responsibility for their learning if they can clearly see what needs to be done and, crucially, why what they are doing and learning during the lesson is important.

One particularly effective way of helping them to do this is to use a learning continuum.[1] This shows students that learning is a journey and provides a road map for success, showing what they need to do to get to the next stage. It can be used constantly throughout the lesson to monitor progress, helps to keep your objectives 'live' and gives students a vocabulary to use when reviewing and evaluating the progress they are making.

This type of approach also supports differentiation and helps you to demonstrate how your teaching and learning matches individuals' needs. It is also a useful tool for reflecting on how the journey is going, what to do when learners get stuck and what helps learners to make the most progress.

Learners with lower start points are more likely to need support to help them move along the continuum, whereas those who start further along may need additional challenge so that they can go further. It is worth remembering that even those learners who begin at the same start point may need different strategies and support to help them to achieve.

---

1   The idea for the learning continuum comes from Jackie Beere's *The Perfect (Ofsted) Lesson* (2010).

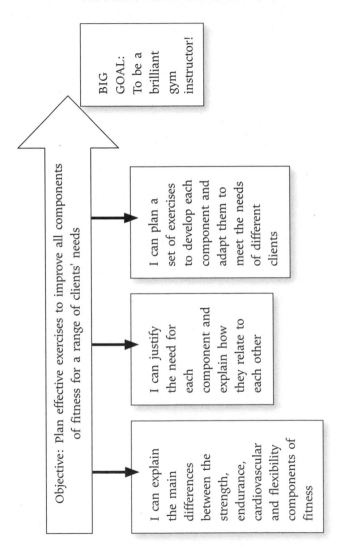

BIG GOAL: To be a brilliant gym instructor!

Objective: Plan effective exercises to improve all components of fitness for a range of clients' needs

I can plan a set of exercises to develop each component and adapt them to meet the needs of different clients

I can justify the need for each component and explain how they relate to each other

I can explain the main differences between the strength, endurance, cardiovascular and flexibility components of fitness

Top tip

■ Do make sure that you pay particular attention to those learners who you know are at risk of achieving less, and plan how to help them make extra progress in every lesson.

Effective differentiation is needed to ensure that your learners make 'better than expected progress given their starting points' (Ofsted, 2014: 47). You need to have a deep understanding of what they already know and can do, and be acutely aware of the progress they are making towards the success criteria so that you can modify and adapt what you are doing in response to what is happening. Learners can be endlessly surprising, so make sure that you continuously challenge any assumptions that you and your learners make about their potential. Starting points might tell us something about where learners are now, but they can be misleading in terms of what learners could potentially achieve.

'Steep learning curves are the right of all students regardless of where they start.'

Hattie (2012): 92

How do we know they are learning?

One of the problems with learning is that it takes place inside students' heads, where it cannot be seen! If learners are going to demonstrate that they are making tremendous progress, they need to be engaged in activities that make their learning visible. For example:

■ Explaining concepts and ideas in their own words.

■ Creating and asking challenging questions.

■ Making connections between different parts of their learning, and between what they are learning and the outside world.

■ Recreating (rather than reproducing) information.

- Offering analogies and interpretations (e.g. 'Oh, yes, it's a bit like when ... when we ...').
- Making and justifying decisions.
- Solving problems and generating alternative ideas and solutions.
- Talking to each other about what they are learning.
- Consciously reflecting on their learning and discussing how to improve it.

We need to know how well they are learning so that we can adjust what we are doing to help them improve. And, of course, it's also what inspectors will be looking for in outstanding lessons!

Assessment *as* learning

'Assessment which is explicitly designed to promote learning is the simple, most powerful tool we have for both raising standards and empowering lifelong learners.'

Assessment Reform Group (1999): 2

When assessment is used as learning, it makes learning visible so that teachers and learners can improve what they are doing. It gives learners the confidence to be wrong and make mistakes. By increasing learners' awareness of what they can do and how they learn, it develops their independence and ability to take responsibility for their own learning.

Assessment *for* learning (AfL) has been around for a while now, and has been defined as: 'the process of seeking and interpreting evidence for use by learners and their teachers to decide where the learners are in their learning, where they need to get to and how best to get there' (Assessment Reform Group, 2002: 2).

Assessment *as* learning extends effective AFL practice and is assessment that students own themselves. It is based on the principle that all students can manage their own learning and improve, thereby enabling them to become expert learners – an essential requirement if they are to thrive in the future.

> 'The illiterate of the 21st century will not be those who cannot read and write, but those who cannot learn, unlearn, and re-learn.'
>
> Toffler (1973): 271

An observer walking into a lesson or workshop where learners are making brilliant progress, as a result of effective assessment as learning strategies, will see:

- Learners who can discuss the lesson objectives and success criteria with confidence and who know exactly where they are and what they need to do to make further progress.

- Teachers who constantly learn from their students by observing, listening and responding to what is happening.
- Teachers and learners who work together to improve the quality of learning.
- Learners who are using and developing the skills of peer and self-assessment to advance their learning, and that of their peers.

This last point is crucial. Peer and self-assessment are essential to great progress as they enable students to improve the quality of their work as they go. Learners can only become truly independent, and take responsibility for monitoring the quality of their own work, when they can competently self-assess. This means that you need to give them plenty of opportunities to practise these important skills.

Self-assessment

'Learners are excellent at assessing their own work, and teachers make particularly good use of this and of peer reviews, to help learners progress and take actions themselves to improve.'

Ofsted (2013a): 8

Learners can only self-assess well if they know exactly what success and good work looks like. If you can, show them a high quality finished product – for example, a completed electrical circuit, decorated cake, worked maths solution or a particularly good response to an essay question. (Awarding body criteria can also be useful, but only if it is translated into language that learners can easily understand.)

Spoof assessment is an excellent way of helping learners to see what truly great work looks like. It can also be used to help them avoid common errors and works very well in both theory and practical workshops.

Case study

Tricia gives her learners extracts from pass and distinction assignments. They have to decide which are passes and distinctions, and why. The pass work often has lots of detail and description but lacks analysis and evaluation, unlike the shorter but more precise distinction work. The learners almost always get it wrong, and this demonstrates (more effectively than telling them) the characteristics of good work.

Case study

Brett's catering students watch a DVD of a great kitchen team in action. They evaluate the performance of the team against criteria they have devised, identifying any additional points they need to include. They use this to evaluate their current strengths and weaknesses and set personal improvement targets. This evaluation is used to determine roles and responsibilities and provides opportunities for learners to improve their skills in the next practical lesson.

Getting learners to devise criteria to evaluate their work can be very powerful, particularly when learners include individual goals. Below is an extract from a self-assessment pro

Criteria	No	Partly	Yes	Comments
I have explained why it is important to respect the rights of others.				
I have given several examples of where I have seen this done at work and at college.				
I have discussed how the way we use language might impact on people from different cultures, and have given positive and negative examples of this.				
I give examples of how I can make sure that I respect the rights of others.				
Personal goal for this assignment: I have made sure that my assignment is logically structured with headings and references.				

forma used by a business studies teacher. (The student's personal goal appears in the bottom row.) The great thing about this strategy is that it usually improves the quality of work *before* the student does it, significantly speeding up progress.

Learning journals

Learning journals – diaries or logs in which learners reflect on and evaluate their experiences – can help students to develop self-assessment skills. Some students may need prompts to get them started on the right lines – for example:

- What have I learned/what did I get better at (and how do I know)?
- Did I learn anything unexpected? What was it and how did I learn it?
- Next time I am going to focus on ...
- I will know I am improving when I can ...

Many trainers and assessors make particularly good use of learning journals to encourage learners to connect different aspects of their learning, such as on- and off-the-job training, and to help them to reflect on and learn from their work experiences.

Learning journals work best when students use them to develop and monitor their *own* learning goals. Again, they may need support at first to help them create useful and manageable goals, so some prompts might help:

- My learning goals for this (stipulate learning experience) are ...
- I will achieve them by ...
- I will know I have achieved them when I ...

Top tip

- Consider using technology to promote the use of self-assessment. Learners can make use of Twitter, Facebook, a phone diary or your VLE to keep their journal up to date. Pick key themes for them to respond to with Twitter feeds – for example, 'Summarise the top ten things you have learned about web design over the last four weeks.'

Teaching learners the skill of reflection is critical if they are to become good at self-assessment. Consider using questions to prompt their thinking:

- What am I most pleased about?
- When did I feel most confident?
- What did I do when I got stuck?
- What did I find difficult?
- What would have made it better?

■ How can I try to improve this?

■ What do I want to know more about?

Other methods – such as traffic light cards, cups or thumbs-up – are quick, easy and fun ways of finding out how learning is going – for instance:

Thumbs down/red: Not got it.

Thumbs sideways/amber: Got a bit/some of it.

Thumbs up/green: Got it, let's move on.

When learners are working on a task, they can change the colour of their card as they grow more confident or to indicate that they are struggling. These methods always need following up as they may not be completely accurate or honest – for instance: 'That's great, I'm really pleased we've all got it! Jodie, can you explain *exactly* what we mean by gaseous diffusion.'

Peer assessment

Effective peer assessment is an essential component of your perfect lesson. When this works well, your learners will demonstrate remarkably high levels of personal, social and employability skills – and any observer will not fail to be impressed. Of course, this is not going to happen overnight. Learners need to develop their skills through coaching, repetition and practice. There also needs to be a culture of support and collaboration where students:

- ▨ Understand that making errors and getting it wrong is an important part of learning, and appreciate the opportunity to learn from their own and each others' mistakes.

- ▨ Support each other to improve because they know how important they are to each others' learning, and that they need to work together to ensure that everyone makes progress.

- ▨ Know how to give constructive and helpful feedback to each other, and how to accept and use feedback from others.

- ▨ See you modelling the skills of good dialogue so they know what supportive dialogue looks and feels like.

- ▨ Show respect for each others' efforts and work, listen carefully to each other and understand that mockery and disrespect will not be tolerated.

What follows are two ideas for peer assessment activities that teachers have used to great effect in theory and practical sessions.

Learning circuit

Learners complete a task either as a group, in pairs or individually. Partway through, on a signal from you, they get up and move to their peer's work to identify what they are doing well and make suggestions for improvement. (Do this a few times so they get to see as much other work as possible.) They then improve their own work based on the advice they have been given. This is a powerful strategy because, in addition to feedback from their peers, they also encounter new ideas to further improve their work.

Feedback prompts

These are tools to help learners make constructive comments about the work they are reviewing. Adapt these or create your own prompts with your learners:

- ▓ I thought this was good because ...
- ▓ I think this could be even better if you ...
- ▓ I wanted to ask you why ...
- ▓ I was really interested in ...
- ▓ I would like to use this idea in my own work because ...
- ▓ I would like to give you this (student's own idea). I think you would like it because ...
- ▓ MOT: More of This would help because ...

For example:

'I wanted to ask why you had picked those diseases to focus on.'

Or

'I thought this could be even better if you explained why you thought polio was more serious than tuberculosis.'

Getting learners into the habit of *asking* for feedback from peers encourages them to take more responsibility for their learning, and can help learners to evaluate their progress towards individual goals. This works particularly well if learners identify at the start of a learning session what they would particularly like feedback on, and then link this to their individual goals.

Case study

Lucy asks her learners to turn the lesson objectives into a mind map and write their individual goals against each of the objectives. She also asks them to identify at least one additional personal, social or employability goal. Learners then share their goals with a nominated peer and work together to update and review their progress throughout the lesson.

All peer and self-assessment activities need to include an element of what Jackie Beere refers to as DIRT, or Dedicated Improvement and Reflection Time (2012: 29). There is absolutely no point in checking learning (however brilliantly you do it) if it does not improve as a result. Make sure you always create space for this in your workshop or lesson so that you can dazzle inspectors when they evaluate students' understanding of 'what they have to do to improve their skills and knowledge, which is checked and reflected in subsequent tasks and activities' (Ofsted, 2014: 52).

Great questioning for brilliant learning

> 'I suggest that there are only two good reasons to ask questions in class: to cause thinking, and to provide information for the teacher on what to do next.'
>
> Wiliam (2011): 78

Great questioning is one of the most powerful teaching tools at your disposal. Done well, it can ensure learners make great progress by:

- Helping learners to make connections between what they already know/can do and what you want them to know/be able to do.
- Increasing the depth, quality and complexity of their learning.
- Finding out what they are learning and how they are thinking.
- Promoting and improving the development of practical skills.
- Encouraging reflection on the learning process.
- Providing access to learners' minds and ways of thinking.

Activity/Bloom level	Verbs	Question stems
Creating/synthesising This is about learners creating, inventing, designing, problem solving, etc.	Imagine, generalise, relate, predict, conclude, combine, modify, rearrange, substitute, plan, design, create, compose, formulate, prepare, generalise, rewrite	How would you design a ... to ...? How would you do ... differently with a new client? Explain what might be a possible solution to ...? What would be your way of dealing with ...? What would happen if ...? How many ways can you ...? How would you create new/different uses for ...? What is the best way of developing a proposal that would ...? How would you go about making a new recipe for ...? How could you use this in ... situation?

| **Evaluation** This is about learners making decisions, taking a stand and making judgements. | Test, measure, rank/ grade, discriminate between, assess, verify, judge, decide, select, choose, recommend, convince, support, summarise | What would be a better solution to ...? How would you judge the value of ...? How can you justify your decision to ...? How would you have handled ...? What would you recommend and why? How effective are ...? How could you have done that more efficiently? What changes to ... would you suggest? How would you feel if ...? How effective are ...? What do you think about ...? |

Activity/Bloom level	Verbs	Question stems
Analysis This is when you want learners to look for underlying principles and the relationships between different aspects of a concept or topic.	Analyse, identify, recognise, see patterns, select, order, organise, classify, arrange, separate, divide, explain, connect, compare, contrast, infer	Which events could have happened when ...? How was this similar to ...? What are other possible outcomes? What was the underlying theme of ...? What were the motives behind ...? Why did these changes occur? What will happen if you change this part of the process? Can you explain what happened when ...? How is X similar to Y? What are some of the problems of ...? Can you distinguish between ... and ...? What is/was the problem with ...?

'The skilful use of questioning enables teachers to check students' knowledge and understanding and to challenge students to improve their work further.'

Ofsted (2013b): 3

Use questions at the top end of Bloom's taxonomy to encourage the development of analysis, evaluation and synthesis skills. The table that follows shows examples of activities, verbs and question stems, which have been collated and adapted from a range of sources, including Jackie Beere (2012) and the Excellence Gateway Treasury (n.d.).

Brilliant questions are not likely to spring to mind just when you need them, so it makes sense to plan what you might want to ask learners in advance. Some teachers create a prompt sheet of higher order question stems and keep it handy during the lesson. This can come in really useful when you need to give learners an extension activity or further challenge. The more you practise asking great questions, the better you will get.

You might think that progress is more obvious in practical workshops and the workplace, because teachers or observers can actually see what learners are doing, but this is only part of the story. Learners need to be able to demonstrate the thinking processes that underpin their practical skills and show where and how they are making links between theory and practice. Great questions help learners to make those connections, and challenge them more deeply.

Case study

Rob's hairdressing learners are working on clients in the salon. As they work, Rob asks them questions such as:

- Are you going to use the texturising or thinning scissors?
- How did you decide that graduation would work best for this client?
- How else could you create volume?
- What else do you need to do before you apply the colour?
- How do you know that this will work?

These questions are all designed to help learners to articulate their thinking in relation to the practical activities, and provide Rob with useful information about their levels of understanding.

Case study

During Ahmed's circuit training workshop, he asks learners to identify what is happening in their bodies, getting them to name muscles, joints and energy systems. He also asks a range of questions that require analysis and synthesis, such as: 'How could we change this exercise to isolate the triceps?' or 'What other exercises would work this muscle group?'

Socratic questioning

Socrates was known as a great educator who taught by asking questions. Use Socratic questions when you want to probe depth of thinking, challenge assumptions or determine how well learners understand complex issues. Even better, teach learners how to use Socratic questions themselves to enrich and enhance the quality of their dialogue and discussions.

There are six types of Socratic questions:

1. Asking learners to clarify their thinking: Why are you saying that? Could you explain further? Can you give me an example?

2. Challenging assumptions: Is this always the case? Why do you think that?

3. Probing reasoning and evidence: Why is that happening? What do you think causes ...?

4. Questioning viewpoints and perspectives: Can/did anyone see this another way? Why is this better than ...?

5. Implications and consequences: So, if that happened, what would be the result? How does ... affect ...?

6. Questions about the question: Why do you think I asked that question? Why was that question important? Which one of your questions turned out to be the most useful?

Make sure that you help learners to develop their learning to learn, or metacognitive, skills by asking them questions about learning processes, such as the way they approached tasks, overcame obstacles and the different strategies that worked (or not). Encourage them to ask these questions of themselves too. For example:

■ Why did I do that? (Helps them to understand the thought that led to the actions.)

■ How did I do that? (What strategies led to success – e.g. worked with others, good planning, redrafted, asked for help, got feedback?)

■ How can I do this again/make sure I don't do this again? (This helps them to apply the learning to future work.)

Killer question[2]

Claire Gadsby emphasises the crucial nature of incisive ques
tioning. The 'killer' question worth asking at the end of (and
at key points during) your lesson is: 'What do you know/can
do now that you couldn't when we started?' This is where
your learners should be able to explain enthusiastically and
in great depth what they have learned – and impress an
inspector by demonstrating exceptional development of their
skill and understanding. But don't wait until you are
observed: ask it all the time so that learners get used to
answering the question well. It will improve their ability to
talk confidently about their progress and learning.

Questioning techniques

Creating great questions is one thing, but how you go about
using them in a group setting is another. The way you ask
questions and deal with answers will have a significant
impact on how students respond to and learn from them.
Here are some great ideas for questioning techniques.[3]

---

2   This idea comes from Claire Gadsby's book, *Perfect Assessment for Learning*
    (2012).

3   All of the ideas in this section come from teachers and trainers who have
    used them very successfully, and who have invited me into their lessons to
    see them in action. There are too many to thank individually but, collectively,
    thank you all.

Think, pair, square, share

Think: Learners individually write down their answer to a question.

Pair: They then share their thoughts in pairs, comparing and contrasting answers.

Square: Pairs then team up into fours (depending on numbers) and work together to agree which are the best answers or come up with a group answer.

Share: This can be done in a number of ways. The teacher might take feedback from each group and use this as the basis for discussion or further learning, or learners could peer evaluate each others' answers and compile a class definition.

Pose, pause, pounce, bounce

Pose the question to the whole group.

Pause (at least 10 seconds) to give them time to think.

Pounce on a learner to give the answer.

Bounce the question immediately to another learner, asking them, for instance, if they agree, disagree or to expand the answer.

This strategy keeps all learners on their toes and makes sure all are involved. You can take this a step further by 'bouncing' the answer to the whole class – they can hold up cards or use thumbs to show if they agree/disagree with the answer. You can then pick any learner and ask them to explain why.

Comparing answers

Having set your learners a challenging question (or a few challenging questions), either individually or as a pair, team them up with another learner/pair to compare and improve their answers. They discuss where they have differed in their responses and collaborate to develop a better answer.

Electronic voting systems

Electronic voting systems (EVS) enable learners to use mobile phones or other devices to text or 'vote' their response to questions that you ask verbally or display on the board. They are useful because *all* learners must respond, and can do so individually and simultaneously. This provides you with immediate feedback from the whole class. EVS use usually generates high levels of interest and enthusiasm as learners like using their phones! They will only have an impact on progress, however, if the questions are challenging and the results are used to improve and advance learning.

Learners asking the questions

Encourage students to ask the questions for a change! Getting learners to ask questions of each other is a brilliant way of prompting them to engage deeply with material and take responsibility for their learning. It also means that they will impress an inspector with the quality of their learning. Get your students to use Bloom's taxonomy when creating questions so they know that they are challenging enough.

Top tip

- Ask learners to construct closed questions – for example:
  - The teacher presents learners with a problem linked to the topic being learned (e.g. 'Sales of heavy machinery fell 20% over the last year').
  - To solve this problem, learners have to come up with a series of questions that the teacher will only respond to with a yes or no answer.

This will require careful question planning, involving the prioritising and sequencing of information. It also means that learners have to listen to each other. You can make this into a competition by putting learners into teams and limiting the number of questions they can ask.

Challenge scale

Do your learners know when they are working hard enough and when they are in their comfort zones? Ask them questions to determine how hard they think they are working. This can be linked to a 'challenge scale' like the one below:

1. **Easy:** I can do this without any real effort.

2. **Comfy:** I can do this if I get on with it. It may take a bit of time and I will have to work at it but it won't be hard.

3. **Stretch:** I should be able to do this but I will have to work hard and put in a lot of effort. I might need help.

4. **Strain:** I don't think I can do this. It is too hard and I might give up.

This approach can help you to decide where you need to provide support or additional challenge. It will also demonstrate very nicely to an inspector how hard your learners are working and how well you are responding to individual needs.

Top tips for terrific questions

■ Ask challenging, high order questions that genuinely evaluate the depth and extent of learning (rather than checking that they were listening to what you just said!).

- Engage *all* learners in thinking about and responding to questions.

- Use wait time – give learners time to think about their answers (at least ten seconds) and don't *ever* jump in with the answer yourself. Use supplementary questions if necessary to help them to work it out for themselves.

- Ladder up and down with easier and harder questions, where necessary, to find out how far their learning has got and where any sticking points are.

- Ask questions that evaluate *how* effectively they have learned as well as *what* they have learned.

- Use questions to help learners reflect on all aspects of their learning, such as teamwork, independent learning, persistence, communication and so on.

- Ask questions that help learners to transfer and connect learning from their other lessons, units and prior experiences.

- Use incorrect answers as a great opportunity to develop and improve learning. The way you respond to wrong answers will affect how well learners respond to subsequent questions. If you show learners that it is okay to get it wrong, they are more likely to take risks, participate and think creatively in future.

Feedback and progress

Effective formative feedback is essential to great progress because it enables learners to bridge the gap between where they are and where they need to be. It does this by providing them with specific information about what is and isn't being learned well, compares their performance against clear standards (rather than other students) and, crucially, leads to improvement.

High quality feedback works by focusing attention on what needs to be done to improve. It involves giving learners time to talk about, reflect on and improve the quality of their learning. For feedback to improve learning, students need to absolutely clear about:

- Where they are in their learning.
- Where they need to get to next.
- What improvements they need to make to get there.

Suggestions for improvement should enable students to close the learning gap and encourage them to take responsibility for moving their own learning forward. Make sure that they understand and respond to your feedback – and improve their work as a result.

Feedback is so important to learner progress that it deserves a chapter of its own, so more information on making effective use of feedback can be found in Chapter 6.

Demonstrating progress in maths and English

> 'Teaching and learning develop English, mathematics and functional skills, and support the achievement of learning goals and career aims.'
>
> Ofsted (2014): 49

Take every possible opportunity to develop reading, writing, speaking and listening, ICT and numeracy in your perfect FE lesson. Without these crucial skills, many learners will have difficulty accessing the rest of the curriculum, limiting their ability to make progress and severely restricting their employment opportunities.

> 'A lack of English and maths skills within the British workforce currently poses the biggest threat to the economy of the nation.'
>
> Stephen Kennedy, Skills for Logistics, quoted in Learning and Skills Improvement Service (2009): 2

Some teachers are reluctant to include English or maths tasks in their lessons because learners don't enjoy them or find them difficult. This is precisely why you *should* make them an essential part of your lesson rather than avoiding them. Learners will only get better if they practise. They need to be able to develop literacy and numeracy skills in context, relate them to the 'real' world and see how important they are to their future learning and careers. This means that you need to create frequent and meaningful opportunities for learners to use and improve English and maths in *all* of your lessons – and don't leave it all up to the functional skills tutors!

Top tip

▓ Keep a careful watch out for those learners who do not participate in reading or writing activities. Students who struggle will often develop avoidance strategies, such as getting others to do it for them.

Below are some ideas that vocational teachers have used to reinforce and embed literacy and numeracy in context:

▓ Tell learners you are going to make deliberate mistakes in maths and English during the lesson and they have to spot them (they usually like catching you out doing something wrong!). Have a competition to see who can find the most mistakes.

▓ Ask learners to identify and correct spelling, punctuation and grammar during peer and spoof assessment activities.

▓ Develop maths skills by asking learners to work out the logistics of timings, costings and numbers when planning a wedding, party, sports, coaching or other events.

- Give learners a series of statements and ask them to work out which one is an instruction and why. This usually leads to a good debate around effective communication.

- Give learners some subject-relevant text, but without punctuation. Ask them to punctuate it and summarise the content or answer a question related to the text.

- Provide learners with apostrophe-free materials (e.g. recipes, menus, reports, scenarios) and ask them to work out where the apostrophes should go.

- Ask learners to summarise their learning using a mix of, for instance, descriptive, explanatory and persuasive text. They should then discuss where, how and why they would use these different styles in their future jobs – for example, writing emails to clients or preparing reports.

- A group of childcare learners are asked to create sentences using past, present and future tenses when planning and reviewing play activities.

- Construction learners are asked to use a wide range of maths skills when working out how much plaster is needed to cover an area, costing a job or working out how to mix different ratios. Afterwards, the teacher asks them to identify all the different techniques to help them recognise the progress they are making.

Have a good look at your lesson plans and schemes of work and identify opportunities to develop and embed these skills. Talk to other teachers about how and when they are doing it. Avoid taking a tick-box approach or doing it just because you 'should'. Learners quickly see through this and may become demotivated if they sense that your heart is not in it, so treat maths and English with the same passion and commitment as your vocational area.

Case study

When Aiza puts her learners into small groups, she often uses technical terms for the group names, for example, Differential, Torquing, Carburettor and Centrifugal. She asks learners to write down the word individually before sharing their spellings and understanding of what the word means. This reinforces their ability to spell important words and understand technical terms. Sometimes she will ask them to give each other group names – then they come up with the most difficult word or term that they can think of!

Here are some ideas for demonstrating progress in lessons.

Temperature check

At the start of the lesson, students write their names on a sticky note and place it a wall thermometer showing confidence levels (ranging from very confident to quite confident to not confident) related to a skill or knowledge. Students get up and move their sticky note when they make progress during the lesson.

Pulse points

These are points where you stop the lesson to give learners a chance to think about the progress they are making and, on this basis, decide what should happen next. You can do this at any time during the lesson, including partway through an activity. The aim is to find out what is going on and adjust if necessary. For example, you might ask students to stop and have a sixty-second think on their own about how their learning is going right now. They can then discuss this in pairs, decide what is going well and what needs to be done to improve their learning.

Top tip

■ Use pulse points when an observer arrives partway through a learning session. This will give you a chance to relax, draw breath and will neatly demonstrate the progress your learners have already made and how you are meeting their individual needs.

Concept mapping

Students draw a concept map that demonstrates their learning by individually brainstorming all the key concepts/ideas/information they can recall from the topic or lesson so far. They identify and highlight areas where they are confident and those where they are unsure or are having trouble understanding. This is then discussed and used as the basis for improving learning during the lesson. Learners update their maps throughout the lesson and use them to evaluate progress at the end. The maps can also be used to recap and connect learning.

Scaling

Ask learners to use mini-whiteboards or scoring sheets to score their understanding against the lesson objectives at the start of the lesson (on a scale of 0–8). Regularly update these during the lesson, and ask students to explain to you and each other why they have changed their score.

Talk partners

Getting learners to articulate their learning can be very powerful. You could ask them to get together at key points during a workshop or lesson and ask them to discuss – for example:

- Three key things they have learned.
- What they found easy.
- What they found difficult.
- What they now need or want to learn.

KWL (Know, Want, Learned)

KWL is a brilliant tool for demonstrating progress, and you can use the basic principle of this activity in lots of different ways. It works just as well in practical workshops and workplace learning as it does in classrooms, as it can be done individually or in groups.

At the start of a lesson or workshop, learners identify:

1. What they already know or can do in relation to the topic.

2. What they need, want to know or want to be able to do.

3. What they have learned.

They do the first two at the start of the lesson and fill in the third as they go along (perhaps during pulse points). This works best if they update all three areas throughout the lesson, as learners often get increasingly curious about a topic.

You can make this task very lively and kinaesthetic by getting learners to write on sticky notes and grouping them into categories. This will give you a fabulously visual image of the learning that is going on, and it is incredibly rewarding to watch the changing patterns as learners make progress and move their sticky notes around.

Top tip

One teacher has adapted KWL by using green, orange and red sheets of paper. Learners write what they confidently know on the green sheets, what they know a bit about on the orange sheets and what they don't yet know on the red sheets. They update the sheets throughout the lesson, significantly increasing the amount of writing on the green sheet as they progress.

Key to most of these strategies for demonstrating progress in lessons is that they identify and build on prior learning. Establishing learners' true starting points, and knowing how this differs for individuals, is essential to ensuring that all learners are genuinely making progress. We also need to constantly re-evaluate our assumptions about where learners are starting from. Students learn from their jobs and experiences in the outside world – therefore, we need to bring this new and evolving learning (including the many errors and misconceptions that may accompany it) into our lessons so that it can be built on, shared and improved.

Excellent endings

The plenary is the crucial moment of truth when you find out exactly how far learners have travelled towards the objectives and where there are any remaining gaps.

Don't ever skip this part of your lesson. This is your opportunity to reveal the brilliant progress that students have made and to plan the next steps in the learning. If all learners have not made the progress that was expected, make sure you acknowledge this and discuss it with them, so that they are clear about what will happen next to make sure that they *do* learn what is required.

Top tip

■ Students often learn things we didn't expect them to, so it is crucial that this unanticipated and frequently valuable learning is made visible. This means that plenaries should, as far as possible, be student led so that they have the chance to demonstrate the richness and extent of their learning.

Be sure to have a grand finale to your lesson by creating excitement and enthusiasm about the next one. So that the learners leave feeling motivated and optimistic, give them a feel of what they will be doing next, how it builds on what they have been learning up to now and how it relates to their bigger goals.

Here are some useful ideas for excellent endings.

Countdown 3, 2, 1

Students identify:

3 most important things they have learned.

2 skills they have used and developed.

1 question they've still got about the topic.

Learning chains

Learners individually create a visual image with interlocking shapes that show:

- What I learned today (key points).
- This links with ... (e.g. other topics, lessons, functional skills).
- Skills I used ... (e.g. personal, social, employability, academic).
- How can I use these skills in other areas (transferability).
- What do I need to do to learn better next time?

This technique focuses on skill development. Learners share chains with each other and action plan how they will take learning forward.

Next, the students should answer the following questions:

1. What questions can I now answer about (the topic)?
2. What questions have I still got about (the topic)?

Ask students to summarise their learning by creating a newspaper headline or updating their Facebook status, tweet or blog – you can do this with or without computers.

Sticking points

Students write up their key learning point on sticky notes, using a different note for each point. They also write down what they are still stuck on or confused about. They then work as a whole group or in smaller groups, depending on numbers, to categorise the notes and identify common themes in terms of what has been learned well/less well. This information can then be used to plan the next learning session.

Mini-plenaries

Use mini-plenaries throughout the lesson, at the end of an activity or whenever you think it might be useful to take the 'learning temperature'. This not only helps you to find out how learners are doing, but it also means that an observer can see just how well you are helping all individuals to make progress.

Checklist for great progress every lesson

Ensure that the gap between where learners are at the start of the lesson, and where they need to be at the end, is made clear and that learners know exactly what they have to do to close it.

Make sure that learners have the chance to develop and demonstrate skills – such as teamwork, problem solving and communication – through active and collaborative learning. This is vital. An observer can only see great skill development and progress taking place if learners get a chance to show what they can do.

Embed assessment as learning strategies throughout your lesson and, where possible, use peer and self-assessment strategies to give learners responsibility for advancing and evaluating their learning.

Use great, challenging questions that require *all* learners to think about the answers, demand the use of higher order thinking skills, and which probe and extend learning.

Take the 'learning temperature' frequently throughout your lesson to find out how learners are progressing and what needs to be done to improve the extent or rate of progress.

- Make sure that feedback helps learners to see how well they are doing in terms of making progress towards the learning outcomes. Ensure that you give feedback on the processes and strategies they are using.

- Always end the lesson with a memorable plenary that gives learners the chance to evaluate the progress they have made and to identify the next steps in learning.

Chapter 5
Collaborative Learning that Delivers Results

Effective collaboration improves learners' behaviour, confidence, attitudes to others and can dramatically advance learning.

Collaborative activities enable learners to work independently from you, and to demonstrate and develop:

- High levels of resilience, confidence and independence when they tackle challenging activities.
- Enthusiasm for, participation in and commitment to learning.
- High levels of engagement and interest.
- Exceptional development of skills and understanding.
- The ability to apply skills and background knowledge to great effect.
- The development of speaking, listening and negotiating skills.[1]

Collaborative learning techniques also give you the chance to show an observer how well you:

- Foster good relations and are sensitive to, and promote, equality of opportunity.
- Inspire and challenge all learners and enable them to extend their knowledge, skills and understanding.
- Check learners' understanding effectively throughout learning sessions.
- Deepen learners' knowledge and understanding.
- Promote the development of independent learning skills.
- Take every opportunity to develop crucial skills successfully.

---

1 Adapted from Ofsted's 'outstanding' descriptors for teaching, learning and assessment (2014: 54–55).

Top tip

▪ It really is good to talk – particularly if you are a teenager! The growing use of social media means that teenagers, in particular, talk to each other much less than they used to, so the more opportunities you can give them to practise their communication skills by engaging in purposeful conversation with each other, the better.

Working collaboratively improves learners' understanding and acceptance of each other and encourages them to actively participate in, monitor and take responsibility for their own learning. This is essential in a fast-changing world where the ability to learn, change and adapt is one of the most important skills of all.

Students usually enjoy working together and often achieve more than they would have done alone. Energy, enthusiasm and engagement levels tend to rise dramatically when teachers instigate pair or group work.

However, it is crucial to ensure that all learners actually do make progress when working together. Just putting them into groups does not necessarily lead to effective learning. Learners need to be clear about what they are supposed to be learning and what they will gain by collaborating. They also need to know how to work together effectively if group work is to be successful.

Below are some tips for making sure that collaborative learning really does deliver results.

Developing teamwork skills

The ability to work well as part of a team is highly valued by employers. Skills such as communication, empathy, listening, negotiating, persuasion and conflict resolution make for better lives as well as improved job prospects. Students need time to practise and improve these skills, alongside feedback that tells them how well they are progressing.

Top tip

Good communication and teamwork skills are essential for life and work, and these can only be developed if learners are able to practise and improve them. Teach these skills to learners and make sure that they are explicitly used and evaluated during collaborative activities.

Ensure that learners know that challenge and disagreement are normal when working collaboratively and that it is only by experiencing and overcoming these difficulties that they will learn how to improve their teamwork skills. It is worth teaching learners about the four stages of group work: forming, storming, norming and performing (for more information, see Tuckman,

1965). This helps them to understand what is happening, so that they can work through and resolve issues themselves.

The figure below outlines some features in each of the four stages.

Forming

Learners work out how they fit into the team, what their roles and responsibilities are and what they need to do.

Storming

Differences emerge. Students may challenge each other and disagree about what needs to be done and how to do it. Focus on the task may be lost.

Norming

Learners reach consensus and agree who does what and how things should be done. The group starts to work together to achieve the aims.

Performing

Learners focus on the task. They work independently of the teacher and support each other. They are aware of *how* they are working together as well as what they are aiming to achieve.

Learners need to understand that the main purpose of teamwork is to ensure that every member of the group makes progress, and to recognise that they are all collectively responsible for this. Learners can easily become fixated on completing the task and forget that everybody needs to learn and develop. For example, if a group are choreographing a dance sequence, but one learner does most of the work, it doesn't matter how good the routine is, the group will have failed in their primary aim of *all* making progress in the skill of choreography.

> 'Tutors foster a work ethos strongly focused on respect, teamwork and learning from each other, resulting in very productive and supportive learning communities.'
>
> Ofsted (2013c): 6

If learners are not used to working together, start them off in pairs to build confidence and trust before they work in larger groups. Increase the length and complexity of activities as they get more skilled at working with each other.

Some other ideas for helping students to learn how to work in groups include:

- Talk tokens. Each learner has a set of 'talk tokens' and they use one every time they speak. Once their tokens are gone, they aren't allowed to speak again during the task. However, learners *must* use all their tokens.
- Speed talk. This works well when learners have spent time working on something individually first. Each group

member has, say, thirty seconds to explain their ideas to the others. As each person is talking, another learner takes notes. (The note-taking role is rotated – for example, when student A is talking B takes notes, and when B is talking C takes notes.) At the end of the round, learners summarise what is in their notes and the group use this as a starting point for the task. This works particularly well because it ensures every learner contributes, is heard and participates.

▧ Individual goals. At the start of a collaborative activity, learners identify and share their personal goals in relation to the development of teamwork skills – for example, 'Today I am going to try to listen more carefully to what others are saying.' As the group work together, they help each other to develop these skills by providing feedback and opportunities to practise. At the end of the activity, progress towards these goals is reviewed and new targets agreed.

▧ Observing learning. When learners are working in groups, watch closely how they are working, and note down what you see happening – for example, when they use good skills or work to overcome an obstacle. Feed your observations back to them either during the activity (so they can improve as they go) or at the end. Once you have modelled this once or twice, get the students to do it instead of you.

▧ Learners often need exemplars to help them to agree or disagree constructively with each other. For example:

  ● I think that is a good point because ...

- I don't think that will work because …
- I am not sure about that idea because …

Negotiating and agreeing team rules

Teams will benefit from creating and agreeing a set of rules that set out how they should behave when working together. Although these will probably need to be revisited frequently to start with, working in this way will eventually become routine and learners will consistently be able to collaborate well.

Here are some examples of ground rules that were created by a group of students on a BTEC agriculture course:

- Everybody has to give ideas and say what they are thinking.
- We will listen carefully to each other when we are talking and will respond to what has been said.
- We will wait until someone has finished talking before we speak.
- If we disagree, we must be honest and say so, but we cannot make rude or negative comments about each others' ideas and contributions.
- We will help each other all the time, especially if someone is stuck or finding the work hard.
- We will work really hard together so that our group does really well.
- If we get stuck, we will try to sort it out ourselves before we ask for help.

Case study

A group of hairdressing students were experiencing difficulties with a few overenthusiastic learners who unintentionally dominated discussions. After discussing the problem, the group initiated a yellow/red card system similar to those used during football matches. A yellow card was a warning that the student was overstepping the mark and a red card meant that they were 'sent off' for a period of five minutes during which they could only listen and not speak. This worked exceptionally well, and because the yellow card helped learners to recognise counterproductive behaviour, the red card was rarely used. The teacher extended this idea to other groups. The cards were also used when a learner breached one of the group rules.

Making sure that all learners make progress

The whole point of collaborative learning is that it results in learners making brilliant progress. So, you need to know exactly what progress is being made, who is making it and, critically, where progress is slow or non-existent. The wonderful thing about group work is that it allows you to do this easily and effectively because you are free to facilitate.

Top tip

■ Don't talk to the whole group whilst they are working. This can be annoying and distracting. If you must do this for any reason, stop the activity, get their attention and say what needs to be said quickly and clearly.

Your job, once the activity is under way, is to support, redirect, focus, challenge, provide/elicit feedback and referee. You need to be acutely aware of every single learner and, in particular, those whose learning might be at risk during group activities – for example, students with poor social skills, quiet or disruptive learners or those who prefer to work alone. Pay close attention to these individuals, but make sure that you are also capitalising on the expertise of those with prior learning and experience, and stretching stronger learners. Above all, don't wait until the end of the activity to find out how well they are learning and, if necessary, intervene to review, consolidate and demonstrate progress.

The challenge is, of course, to be able to do all of this without actually interfering with the needs of the group to work independently. So, intervene cautiously and, when you do so, make sure that it is genuinely in the interest of learning.

Top tip

■ Whenever possible, get students to represent and summarise their learning visually as they work. This can be done in a number of ways, such as concept maps, graphic organisers or drawings. The point is that you want their thinking to be evident so that you (or an inspector) can clearly see what progress they are making.

To demonstrate that teamwork has added value and that your learners have made exceptional progress, your perfect lesson must include a discussion and debrief following group tasks. This will help students to understand that the success of their team, and therefore their individual attainment, relies on the full participation of others. This can be achieved by asking reflective questions, such as:

■ What did you do that helped the team to learn?
■ What more could you have done to help the team?
■ What did the team do well?
■ What could the team have done better?

Other questions that will help to demonstrate great progress and the transferability of skills include:

■ What progress did I make with my teamwork skills (and how do I know)?

- What progress did I make in my subject skills and knowledge (and how do I know)?
- What would have made it better?
- What could have made it worse?
- What problems did the group encounter and how did we solve them?
- What is the most important thing I learned about teamwork?
- Where else can I use and practise what I learned today?

This process also helps learners to develop the skills of learning to learn, as they will become increasingly skilled in the process of reflection and evaluation.

Summarising and sharing outcomes from group work

Group work usually produces tangible results that learners want to share with each other. However, levels of interest and participation can often wane after the first couple of groups have presented their findings. Help learners to maintain focus and enthusiasm by making this part of the activity as challenging and stimulating as the original task. Here are some suggestions.

Learners assess each others' work

This keeps them alert and attentive as they need to provide feedback to peers. Here is an example that was used with hospitality learners who had worked together to plan an event.

Case study

Esmae gives each group a different question to use to evaluate their peers' work – for example, group A has question 1, group B question 2 and so on.

1. How well does the plan meet the aims of the task brief (give strengths and weaknesses)?

2. How well does the plan meet the needs of all guests (including those with dietary and access needs)? What more could be done?

3. What licences, approvals and permissions do they need to check or seek before this can go ahead? What are the risks?

She asks learners to provide written and verbal feedback to their peers following the presentation, after which the question is rotated round to a different group.

One-minute feedback

A spokesperson from each group has to summarise what they have done and learned in a minute or less. This helps learners to be concise and clear in their explanations. Allocate a member of another team as timekeeper so you don't have to do it. After each person has spoken, the other teams have a minute to come up with one good question to ask the presenting group.

Home and away

Learners go 'away' to visit each others' groups for a set time to find out what their peers have learned. This means the other learners have to stay at 'home' to explain their work. Swap the roles around partway through. Afterwards, learners reconvene in their home groups and update and improve their own work based on what they have found out from their peers.

Organising the teams

The way you group students for activities can have a huge impact on their learning, so it should be planned carefully in the context of what you are trying to achieve. Most learners will prefer to work in friendship groups – however, this can reinforce assumptions and create prejudices. Students need to learn how to work with a wide range of people, including those whose beliefs and attitudes are fundamentally different from their own. Mixing groups up means that they can learn to relate to each other in a productive way, so do it from day one to get them used to it.

Top tip

Teachers sometimes tell me that the reason they don't mix learning groups is because students complain about it and often don't work well with others. This is exactly why you should do it! There are very few jobs out there where learners can pick and choose who they work with, so it is absolutely essential for their future lives and careers that they learn how to work well with others.

Learners can be grouped randomly or carefully selected, depending on what you want to achieve:

- Putting noisy/dominant learners together and quieter learners together can work well if you want to make sure that everyone gets a chance to be heard.
- Learners who are working on the same task in practical workshops can collaborate to share ideas and solve problems – for example, some learners might be soldering a joint and others fitting waste pipes.
- Mixed or similar ability groups? As a rule of thumb, mixed groups are more effective because learners can teach and learn from each other. Be very careful if you decide to

group learners by ability. Students usually understand this and you run the risk of reinforcing low expectations.

Sometimes it is useful to mix and match groupings. Here is how one teacher did it with great success.

Case study

Ellen's group of media students are about to start filming for their project. Ellen knows that some of her learners are highly skilled in camera use, whereas others are novices. She ask them to self-select which group to work in:

A. I can get on with this right away and don't need any help.

B. I need a bit of help to get me started.

C. I need a lot of help to get me started.

Once they have chosen their groups, she sends group A off with the task sheet and works with the other two until they can get started. At the end of the filming task, she brings everyone back together and mixes the groups up. In this way, they can share what they have done and learned, and the more skilled learners can show the others what can be achieved.

The significant aspect of this approach is that the learners self-assess their starting points. Through effective streaming and mixing, Ellen was able to accelerate the learning of the less skilled students so that they made good progress alongside their peers.

Allocating students roles in group work is a great way of helping learners to understand and experience the different roles that people perform in teams and why they are important. They can follow this up with reflection on how well they carried out the different roles. You can allocate responsibilities to learners or they can decide for themselves. However you do it, make sure that they all get a chance to take on different roles over time.

Some ideas for roles within teams include:

- **Assessor:** checks everybody has a good understanding of what has been learned.
- **Scribe:** summarises key points, checks others agree and clarifies that they have not missed any key information.
- **Coach:** asks great questions to help others see what they are learning and gives feedback on how well they are doing.
- **Leader:** makes sure they complete the task on time, that everybody has had a say and been heard, and participates, delegates and organises if necessary.
- **Engagement chief:** ensures all participate fully. Asks questions to re-engage or directly asks for more contributions from individuals.

■ **Tracker:** keeps the group on track if it looks like they are going off at tangents or are unlikely to achieve the aims.

Responsibilities need to be agreed according to the group and the requirements of the task. Merge, mix and create different roles to suit your aims. Better still, get the learners to decide what is needed for different tasks.

Top tip

■ Group work can highlight differences between students. This can be used positively to close the gap between those who are further ahead or have different experiences and backgrounds.

Making collaboration work in practical workshops

Instigating collaborative work is often tricky in practical workshop situations where learners are, by necessity, working on individual tasks – but don't let this stop you. Students learn better and make better progress when they feel included, respected and socially stable, and teamwork is essential for this.

Embed the spirit and ethos of collaboration in your workshops by:

1. Bringing learners together at the beginning of the session to:

   ● Share what they are going to be working on and what they are trying to achieve.

   ● Give each other hints and tips on how to go about it.

   ● Identify who is going to buddy and support who if they need help at any point.

   ● Identify who they will check their work with before they get the teacher to have a look.

   ● Set up a challenge for learners to decide how they can help each other to make sure that everybody achieves (or exceeds) their aims.

2. Bringing learners together during the session (where appropriate) to:

   ● Solve a problem that one or two learners may be experiencing.

   ● Review/consolidate progress to date and share any key learning or issues.

   ● Identify what still needs to be done and how it will be achieved.

   ● Identify what the team needs to do better to secure progress for everybody.

3. Bring learners together at the end of the session to:

- Review progress against individual targets and objectives.
- Reflect on how well they worked and how effectively they supported each other.
- Give feedback to each other on what they did well and how to improve.
- Identify next steps in learning and how to work together in the next workshop.

This can be done in small groups or with the whole group, depending on what would be most helpful.

Of course, collaborative activities will also demonstrate to an inspector the wonderful progress your learners are making in the development of their personal, social and employability skills.

A significant amount of learning takes place outside of the classroom environment, through work placements, shadowing and mentoring, trips and visits to industrial and working environments and, of course, apprenticeship employment. This has increased with the introduction of study programmes, traineeships and the expansion of apprenticeships.

Learners sometimes find it difficult to see the workplace as a learning environment but, managed well, the potential for extending and accelerating progress is massive. Encourage learners to capitalise on these rich and diverse experiences by discussing and evaluating them in your lessons and workshops. Encourage them to share knowledge and learning with their peers and to reflect on the effectiveness of their on-the-job learning strategies.

Understanding the context that students are working in can help you to personalise their learning and strengthen the connections between their different learning settings and experiences.

Ideas for effective group work

There are many different and creative ways to organise group work, and it is important that you choose the method that is most likely to meet your aims. Some ideas for group work that have been used very successfully include:

Broken information

Students are given information about a topic that is broken down into headings and presented on separate cards. The learners share the cards out so that they all have more or less the same number.

The group then has to complete a task that requires them to make sense of the information – for example, 'Summarise the key functions of the endocrine system, and how it affects massage treatments' or 'What are the key factors that led to the failure of this company, and what should they have done differently?'

The summary task has to be extremely challenging or they will just repeat back the information on the cards. This works particularly well when students have to create a visual representation of their learning.

Jigsaw

The class is split into three smaller groups and each group is given a subtopic to become 'experts' in – for example, group A learn about arteries, B veins and C capillaries.

When they are reasonably confident about their topic, the expert groups split up and form into new (jigsaw) groups which have at least one expert from each subtopic.

Expert learners then teach each other what they have learned. It is important that students know that you will check their learning in *all* topics, so that they pay attention to each other and help one another to learn well.

Outside the box[2]

Learners are given a box containing questions about the topic they are studying. They take it in turn to take a question out of the box to answer. Peers then help each other to improve the quality of their answers.

---

2   Thanks to Tony Kurk for sharing this with me, and demonstrating it in action with his leadership and management students.

In this example, business students are asked questions about a case study they have been working on.

- Describe it. Explain in detail how ExecuCar went from being one of the smallest to one of the largest car hire companies in the US in less than two years.
- Analyse it. What were the main strategies used to drive the expansion and what long-term problems did they cause for the business?
- Apply it. Which UK companies have experienced fast growth recently and what strategies did they use to achieve this?
- Take a stand. Do you think it is better to achieve fast growth in a short period or grow slowly and steadily over time?
- Reinvent it. If you had a small company that you wanted to grow quickly, how could you do this using a different model to the one ExecuCar used?
- Choose a different perspective. If you were a shareholder in ExecuCar, how would you have argued against the expansion plan? How would you have got the other shareholders to agree?

This type of activity can be used to help learners see what is meant by different terms, such as analysis and application, and can significantly improve their vocabulary for learning.

Card sorting

Challenging learners to sort cards into different categories can be great fun and can also lead to powerful learning outcomes. This technique is used frequently in, for example, architecture and web-based design industries.

Sets of cards can be used to introduce new topics or consolidate and review learning. Students can be asked to do tasks such as matching, ranking, classifying, comparing and so on. The tasks can be open ended and exploratory (e.g. 'Sort these cards into categories – you decide what the categories should be') or closed (e.g. 'Match these definitions to the words'). Open-ended tasks prove more challenging but are easier to differentiate. Increase the difficulty of closed activities by including additional 'red herring' cards or definitions that look very similar.

Checklist for making collaborative learning work

■ Set well-defined goals and objectives for group activities which include the development of teamwork skills as well as subject expertise. Learners need to be clear about what is expected of them during and after the activity, and why working as a team is important to their learning. Make sure they know that success depends on how well they work together, over and above achieving the task. Make it clear that every single one of them is expected to contribute fully to the group activity and that they are responsible, collectively and individually, for the success (or otherwise) of the group.

- Build learners' skills and confidence in teamwork by teaching them how team roles and dynamics work. Ensure they have frequent opportunities to develop and improve their skills through practice, coaching, reflection and feedback.

- Cultivate the emotional climate for group work by creating an ethos of safety and support for each others' learning. Learners are much more likely to persist and work hard to overcome challenge and difficulty if they feel they are all 'in it together' and if there is absolutely no fear of failure. Reinforce the importance of this by providing feedback to learners when they demonstrate supportive and inclusive behaviour and work together to resolve problems and issues. Make sure stronger learners have the opportunity to experience difficulties and errors as much as anybody else.

- Manage group work effectively by letting learners do as much as possible for themselves, including resolving any problems with the group or the task. If you need to intervene, do so in a way that gives them the opportunity to put it right for themselves by asking questions that help them reflect on what is happening and make decisions about what they need to do. Try not to answer their questions unless it is with another question. Make sure you constantly check on the progress they are making and keep an eye out for any distracted or off-task behaviour. Avoid staying with any one group for too long, as you will be limiting their opportunity to work independently.

■ Evaluate the progress that learners are making by reviewing and consolidating learning at key points during and at the end of the activity. Learners need to be able to clearly articulate the progress they have made in their subject-specific expertise and teamwork skills, and identify what they need to know more about/do better next time.

Chapter 6

Feedback and Marking that Deliver and Demonstrate Progress

> '[T]he most powerful single moderator that enhances achievement is feedback. The most simple prescription for improving education must be "dollops of feedback".'
>
> Hattie (2012): 50

Effective feedback, which should be 'frequent, detailed and accurate' (Ofsted, 2014: 51) and advance learner progress, is a crucial feature of your perfect lesson. Feedback that focuses on what learners need to do to improve, and shows them how to do this, should be evident in all marked work and demonstrated consistently throughout your lesson.

High quality feedback during lessons is absolutely vital if learners are to make brilliant progress. Because it happens 'live', at the point of learning, feedback can correct errors and misconceptions before they become ingrained. Truly great feedback also helps students to become competent self-assessors so that they can evaluate their own progress and make decisions about what needs to be done to improve.

Students quickly learn that we reward what we value. If we praise safe answers and low-level responses, learners have little incentive to take risks, respond to challenging tasks or make their (possibly inaccurate) thinking visible. Praising the time, effort and persistence that learners put into a task, rather than their ability or a successful outcome, helps them to see the importance of their own actions in achieving success and taking responsibility for their learning. Research suggests that this approach can significantly improve students' confidence and self-esteem as well as their performance (see Black and Wiliam, 2002).

Descriptive and informative feedback that is task focused and followed up with a progress question is particularly helpful. For example:

- You worked together really well on that task and listened to each others' ideas. What difference do you think that made?
- You came up with a lot of really creative ideas for the radio programme. Which ones do you think will be the most useful?
- You don't seem to be getting very far with this. What do you think is holding you up?
- Well done, you have worked out what the main points are. Now can you explain why you think they are the most important ones?

▓ I noticed that you when you got stuck, you tried several different ways to solve the problem. That showed me that you are getting much better at working independently. What do you think you could do now?

Consider using the word 'yet' in your feedback to reinforce a growth mindset:

▓ You have not evaluated these aspects yet. What is a good way of doing that?

▓ You have not quite solved the problem yet. What else could you do that would help?

This type of feedback communicates to learners that success is within their reach. This helps to motivate them, particularly when they experience difficulty. It also helps them see how employing effort *effectively* – by setting goals, organising their time, trying different and creative strategies, and sticking with it – will help them to achieve their aims, and that success in learning is not about proving themselves.

> 'It is the closing of the gap between where the student is and where they are aiming for that leads to the power of feedback.'
>
> Hattie (2009): 177

Learners are much more likely to develop resilience if they understand that learning is often difficult. It is the feedback on what learners get wrong, rather than what they get right, that improves learning. So learners need to know that if they are finding tasks easy, then they are not learning anything new. This means that learning activities need to be difficult enough to ensure that *all* learners experience a degree of challenge and have the opportunity to experience failure. If we stop learners from failing, we stop them from learning.

Learners need to know that:

- Getting something wrong or getting stuck is not a problem because that means we can learn – so long as we don't *stay* stuck or wrong.
- Making mistakes is good if we learn why we have made them and how to avoid them next time.
- Learning things properly takes time and we shouldn't expect to get it right straight away.

Engaging learners in highly active, challenging and collaborative activities helps you to find out what impact your teaching is having on their learning. This enables you to give and receive constant, meaningful feedback, and adapt your teaching in real time to meet the needs of your learners.

> 'Opportunities for learners to express their understanding should be designed into any piece of teaching.'
>
> Black and Wiliam (2002): 11

For feedback to improve learning, both you and your learners need to know:

- Where they are now in relation to the objectives and success criteria.
- How well they are working and how effective their learning strategies are in helping them to make progress.
- Where they need to go next – specifically, what aspects of their skills and knowledge do they need to improve?
- How to get there – what steps do they need to take to make sure that they move their learning forward and improve?

Learners need to develop the skills to make these judgements for themselves, so that they become increasingly competent in their learning-to-learn skills.

Focusing feedback on the objectives and success criteria

Make sure your feedback is focused on the objectives and success criteria of the task or lesson. This is important because learners need to understand the reasons for their success or failure, and be able to recognise what quality in their learning looks like. When learners are clear about the aims and goals of their learning, and know what to focus their attention on, they become confident, competent self-assessors who can talk with confidence and clarity about the progress they are making towards their targets and goals and what they need to do to improve.

Providing feedback that moves learning forward

Crucially, feedback needs to be more about improvement than correction if it is to promote learning. Learners must act on suggestions for improvement and be seen to make progress as a result. To do this, make sure that you:

- Give learners one important thing that, if changed, will lead to immediate and noticeable improvement.
- Close the feedback loop by checking that the improvement actions have moved learning forward. Make sure learners show you what they have done to improve and what difference it has made – this makes their progress clearly obvious to them, you and an inspector.
- Be clear with learners about what needs to improve but, where possible, give them choice about how they do it (e.g. 'You need to explain this in more depth' or 'How could you do that?').
- Make time in lessons for learners to act on your feedback and improve their learning, so that you can see what difference it has made.
- Provide feedback that challenges and moves learners on (e.g. 'You have classified the types of operating systems. Now compare and contrast the main advantages and disadvantages of two of them').

■ Consider giving learners descriptive feedback first and then give them time to work out for themselves what they need to do to improve, rather than telling them. This helps them to take responsibility for their learning.

■ Team learners up with 'success partners' whose job it is to help and challenge each other to improve following feedback.

■ Pose a question as feedback (e.g. 'What would improve your explanation?' or 'What other examples of leisure opportunities for older adults could you include?').

Make sure that you provide feedback for all aspects of their learning – the depth and quality of their academic and intellectual development, as well as how effectively they are working as a team and any other personal, social and employability skills that they are (or should be) using.

Using feedback to grow independent learners

Help learners to take responsibility for their learning by genuinely involving them in all aspects of the assessment process. Feedback is only formative when learners actually do something about it and, crucially, they must do this for themselves – we can't do it for them. We need to help learners to develop the skills to accurately and consistently self-monitor, and adjust their learning accordingly.

Put learners in charge of their own feedback by using questions to get them thinking about the quality of their learning, thereby developing the important skill of metacognition.

Don't keep these questions to yourself though – create a set with students that they can use to take ownership of their learning and monitor their own progress. This is essential for learners who do a large proportion of their learning in the workplace.

Some ideas for questions to encourage students to reflect on their own learning are included in the table below.

Where am I going? Enable learners to clarify their goals and what is expected of them.	What exactly do I need to do? Why am I doing this? What do I know about this already? What strategies could I use? How will this be assessed? What options and choices do I have?
How am I going? Help learners to self-evaluate how well they are working and what strategies have been more or less effective. How well are they progressing and what gaps or errors in learning remain?	What is working well/less well? What can I do to make this better? Am I making progress towards the goal? What am I learning? What else could I try? What should have happened/ should it have looked like?

Moving forward This is where learners decide what they are going to do to improve their learning and how they are going to go about it. This includes thinking about how they could use successful strategies elsewhere.	What could I do to improve my work? What difference will that make? What else could I do? (ask this a few times) What would happen if ...? Where else would that strategy/ idea work? What is the first thing I need to do? How will I know if it has worked? What else do I need to do/think about? What help do I need with this?

Make sure that learners respond to any feedback they get from you or their peers by giving them time to talk about, reflect on and improve their learning during lessons. This will enable you to demonstrate how well 'timely information, advice and guidance enable individuals to gain greater learning autonomy and decrease dependence on others' (Ofsted, 2014: 53).

Teaching learners how to get the feedback they need to improve

The ability to ask for the feedback you need is an essential employability skill. Model it yourself and get learners to practise it. Encourage them to ask for feedback from their peers, employers and other tutors, and help them to ask for the right sort of feedback – that is, feedback that helps them to develop and improve rather than just finding out the answer to a question.

Case study

Katy's Level 3 health and social care learners created a set of questions to help them get feedback about their performance during work placements. The learners have already evaluated their strengths and weaknesses, and are now seeking feedback that will help them to make better progress.

The learners created a set of generic questions and then adapted them to suit their work context:

- What is good about my communication with the residents I am working with and what could I do better?

- It is taking me a long time to update my records – what would help me to do this faster whilst still maintaining accuracy?

- How well did I support and protect the dignity of X during the bathing process?

Differentiating through individualised feedback

More than anything else, feedback provides you with the opportunity to stretch those learners who are stronger or further ahead, and support and encourage others to persevere. You need to continuously check where each learner is in relation to the goals of the lesson, and give them accurate, descriptive feedback that *helps each individual* to make progress.

Whilst effective formative assessment helps all learners, it helps the (so-called) low attainers more than the rest, which can lead to a potential narrowing of achievement gaps (Black and Wiliam, 2002).

Try to avoid comparing students with their peers, as this can demotivate those who are further behind and lead to learners trying to prove themselves rather than improve their learning. If you work with the notion of 'personal bests', learners will gain confidence when they compare their progress to their previous point, and see how far they have travelled.

One useful model for differentiated feedback is the 'conscious competence' learning matrix.[1] This can help to identify at what stage a learner is in their development and what type of feedback will be most helpful to them at this point. It is a useful analysis tool, as learners can easily be at different stages for different topics, activities, skills and so on.

---

1   The original source of the unconscious/conscious competence model is unknown – many references go back thousands of years. This model was developed by staff on a teacher education course at Leicester College in 2002.

Unconscious competence

As learners develop skills, good practice becomes a habit. Some adult learners may have good problem-solving skills but are not aware of how useful they are to their learning.

▨ Use feedback to help them recognise and build on prior learning and experiences.

▨ Use feedback to help them to move what is unconscious to the conscious to improve confidence and self-esteem.

Unconscious incompetence

Learners don't yet know what they don't know. This can be particularly difficult if you are trying to change attitudes or behaviours.

▨ Raise their awareness gently by helping them to see what competence looks like.

▨ Aim to help students to realise this for themselves wherever possible.

Conscious incompetence	Conscious competence
Learners know what they cannot yet do and how far they have to go to meet the objectives. This can feel demoralising. ■ Ensure that feedback helps them to clearly see what they need to do and how they can do it. ■ Monitor closely, set interim targets, help them to prioritise and celebrate when they make progress.	This can be a tricky one! ■ Focus your feedback on helping students to take ownership of their learning by getting them to reflect on the skills they have used and developed, and how they can use these again in different situations. ■ Make absolutely sure that they know how they can continue to build on their success and make further progress.

Marking

> 'Marking is an act of love.'
>
> Phil Beadle

Feedback on students' written work needs to be as specific, positive and formative as the oral feedback they receive in lessons. Inspectors will expect to see frequent, high quality and constructive written feedback leading to high levels of engagement (Ofsted, 2014: 55). Marked work should clearly show that learners have improved the quality of their work following feedback.

Most teachers say that they spend far too much time marking. The truth is that far too much teacher time is taken up by marking which has limited, if any, impact on student progress. Research by John Hattie (2012: 50) indicates that:

- Many learners do not read comments on their written work, preferring to compare their grades or marks with others.
- When learners do read comments, they often don't understand what is meant by them.
- Teachers tend to write the same comments time and time again for the same students.
- Students rarely take note of, or act on, the comments they receive.

These are critical issues. If you are going to invest time and effort in marking, you need to be sure that it is going to improve learning and enhance progress. The answer to this is not simply to spend more time marking, but to mark more effectively and efficiently. This chapter outlines some strategies and approaches that will help you to do just that.

Doing more marking with students than you do without them

Making assessment, marking and feedback integral to the learning process by doing it *with* your students increases their confidence and competence as self-assessors, thereby promoting the development of true independence and success in learning. It will also increase the impact of your feedback whilst reducing the amount of time you spend marking. This is because marking with the students narrows the gap between what they and you see as quality work. This improves the standard of the work they submit, giving both of you less remedial work to do.

Here is how one teacher does it.

Case study

Jamil's learners bring a first draft of the whole, or part of, an assignment to the lesson – usually a week or so before the deadline.

Working in pairs, the learners swap their work with another pair for marking. They then mark the work against the assessment criteria using a traffic light framework, where green = good, amber = nearly there and red = needs improving. They also identify any spelling, punctuation or grammatical errors.

Next, the pairs get together as a group of four and help each other to decide how to improve their work based on the feedback they receive and what they have learned from looking at each others' work.

Finally, Jamil asks the learners to summarise the main areas for improvement, their learning from the activity and what needs to be done to secure improvement. The learners then commit to identified actions and to posting their improved assignment work onto the VLE for further peer evaluation before submission.

Jamil's learners *always* bring work with them to these sessions, which are timetabled at regular intervals throughout the year. This is because, after the first time, they realise just how valuable this process is to their learning.

This approach is not the same as 'teaching to the test' or simply giving learners time to do assignments in lessons. Marking *with* students is a powerful strategy because:

- Learners develop and improve their skills of self-monitoring and evaluation, thereby making them able to function more independently.

- Students quickly learn what makes high quality work when they have to deal with issues like poor structure or irrelevant materials from their peers, and become skilled at working with and interpreting assessment criteria.

- It gives learners the confidence and impetus to get going. One of the reasons learners frequently give for not completing assignment work is that they 'don't know where to start'.

- Learners develop their ability to monitor and improve their work whilst they are doing it, enhancing their chances of success and higher attainment.

- Learners improve their understanding of the subject when they explore it through the eyes of another student.

- It helps you to see how effective your teaching has been and what you need to do to improve.

To make this strategy work, you need to make sure that:

- Learners understand how to give constructive feedback to each other (see the feedback prompts on page 93).

- Every learner participates – even those who have not brought work with them (make sure that you have spoof assignments or anonymised work from last year, just in case).

- Learners have a structure for giving feedback – for example, three strengths and three areas for improvement.

- You monitor the work they are doing and support and challenge them with plenty of questions, prompts and advice. They will probably struggle with this the first time they do it, but don't give up. They will get better with practice, just as you did!

- They all know exactly what to do to improve and each one commits to improvement actions following the activity. Make the stakes higher by buddying them up with another learner whose job it is to make sure that they have completed the actions before they hand in their work.

Making time for feedback in lessons

One way of ensuring that learners make progress as a result of marking is to make time in lessons for learners to discuss their feedback and support each other to improve. This makes the marking process more transparent and involves learners as genuine partners in assessment. Sharing work and feedback in this way also engenders a powerful sense of belonging and support, which leads to improved confidence, motivation and learning. It also means that you get to find out just how useful your feedback really is! Make this a regular event in your assessment calendar, and watch your learners fly.

If possible, make use of technology and software to involve learners with assessment and marking. Learners can make use of their VLE or a designated Facebook site to discuss their work and ideas, and give feedback to each other. One teacher insists that his learners post and discuss their work online a week before the deadline, and he participates in the online discussion forums set up for each assignment.

Using comment-only marking

Research shows that when we grade students' work, it has a negative impact on their learning, whereas comment-only feedback significantly improves learning and achievement (Butler, 1998). This means that we should avoid grading unless absolutely necessary and, where possible, give comment-only feedback. This will be difficult on some courses. However, the benefits are well worth it, so aim to reduce the amount of grading you do, even if you cannot eliminate it completely.

Consistently grading work has been shown to demotivate learners who regularly get low grades and can, over time, lead to retention problems and a widening of the achievement gap between those with lower and higher start points.

Some teachers manage to do this by not giving the grade until the learners have completed all the required improvement actions for the assignment or giving grades only at set intervals, such as every four or eight weeks. Whatever you do, manage student expectations by telling them why you are doing it and how it will help to improve their learning.

Everybody can improve, even the best student, so make sure that every single learner gets at least one improvement point on every piece of work. Geoff Petty (2009) uses the concept of 'medal and mission' feedback, where every learner gets a medal for what they have done well as well as a mission telling them what they need to do to improve next time. This sends a powerful message that learning is all about continuous improvement, no matter how good you are. This can help to demonstrate your exceptionally high expectations and that learners' work 'meets or exceeds the requirements of the qualifications, learning goals or employment' (Ofsted, 2014: 44).

Learning from your marking

Students' work reveals as much about our teaching as it does about their learning. There is nothing more disheartening than seeing the same problems crop up repeatedly in assignments. As you mark their work, make notes about any common errors, misconceptions or weaknesses that emerge. This might include the development of generic skills, such as analysis and evaluation, as well as subject-specific knowledge and understanding. Note carefully where frequent errors in maths and English occur and where individuals struggle with their work. Use this information to help plan your next lessons, refocus your teaching, support individuals where necessary and prevent history repeating itself!

Case study

Sally creates a table of the most common and significant errors and strengths in her learners' first assignment. Learners use the list to review their work and decide what actions they will take to remedy errors and/or build on strengths. Learners update their own list regularly and use it to help them with future assignments and with peer and self-assessment activities.

Strength	Action	Error	Action
Good examples from your own experience that make explanations clear and show how well you understand.		You need to make the difference between what is fact and what is opinion much clearer.	
Clear introduction that tells the reader what the assignment is about.		You need to say why the stages of development are important.	

Making sure they always respond to your marking

If learners are going to show that they 'improve their skills and understanding through the review and checking process' (Ofsted, 2014: 52), then you need to make sure that the comments you make on their work not only enable but *require* them to make improvements. One way of doing this is to use 'feed-forward' tasks.

For example, you might ask learners to:

- Provide a different example that illustrates the same principle.
- Rewrite this section evaluating the policy instead of describing it.
- Write the final paragraph again, using your own words this time.

Some teachers make use of feedback frames that help close the 'learning loop' by making sure that students respond to learning-centred feedback. For example:

- What worked well (highlight strengths).
- More of this (occasional strengths that could be extended).
- Even better if ... (a gentle way of identifying weaknesses).
- Answer this question (pose a question that will improve the work when answered).
- My response is ... (the learner identifies what they are going to do to improve).

A feedback frame might look something like this:[2]

Target from last piece of work: Make sure I include real examples in my assignment. *Well done. You used very recent and topical examples – the Yahoo! one was particularly relevant to this work and illustrated some of the difficulties that technology can cause.*
Strengths of this work: *You have conducted a thorough and detailed analysis of how different types of appraisal are used in a wide range of companies.*
Corrections/amendments for this piece of work: *You need to evaluate the different appraisal systems in terms of their strengths and weaknesses, and explain why employers choose different models.*
Learning target (what do you need to learn more about and how will you do it?):
Target for next piece of work (put this at the top of your next assignment):

---

2 This frame was created and used by a teacher at Leicester College, following training by Geoff Petty. A wealth of ideas for assessment pro formas can be found at: <http://geoffpetty.com/>.

The idea is that the student sets their own future targets and the teacher *always* responds to these when marking.

Maths and English

Ensure that you always provide feedback on learners' development of English and maths. You need to be able to demonstrate that 'learners' progress in English, mathematics, language and functional skills is monitored and reviewed, and their work is marked carefully' (Ofsted, 2014: 52).

Highlight errors in spelling, punctuation and grammar relentlessly, but don't always correct mistakes for students as this can lead to dependency. Do make sure, however, that they correct the work, even if it doesn't need to be resubmitted.

Checklist for great feedback and marking

- Make sure that feedback focuses learners on the task and the process of learning rather than just getting the right answer. ☑
- Give learners feedback that helps them to see what they are doing well, so they can not only do more of it but also do it in different situations and contexts. ☑
- Ensure that feedback enables learners to recognise errors, move forward and improve the quality of their learning. ☑

- Involve learners in a dialogue about their learning, so that they become assessment competent and can give as well as receive feedback about how they are doing. ✓

- Give feedback that makes your values absolutely clear and foster a growth mindset by focusing feedback on learning and progress. ✓

- Make sure that you designate time in lessons for learners to respond to your feedback and improve the quality of their learning and work, so that their progress is evident. ✓

- Make sure that learners *always* respond to your feedback. ✓

Teaching is tough for anybody, and whilst teaching in FE is often harder and more complex than in most other settings, it is also hugely rewarding as learners' lives are often changed dramatically for the better. I hope that this book helps you to see that, despite the challenges, providing consistently outstanding learning for all your students is not only worthwhile, but also well within your reach.

References and Further Reading

Assessment Reform Group (1999). *Assessment for Learning: Beyond the Black Box*. Cambridge: Cambridge University Press.

Assessment Reform Group (2002). *Assessment for Learning: 10 Principles. Researched-Based Principles to Guide Classroom Practice*. Cambridge: University of Cambridge School of Education.

Beadle, P. (2010). *How to Teach*. Carmarthen: Crown House Publishing.

Beere, J. (2010). *The Perfect (Ofsted) Lesson*. Carmarthen: Independent Thinking Press.

Black, P., Harrison, C., Lee, C., Marshal, B. and Wiliam, D. (2002). *Working Inside the Black Box: Assessment for Learning in the Classroom*. London: NFER Nelson.

Black, P. and Wiliam, D. (2002). *Inside the Black Box: Raising Standards through Classroom Assessment* (London: GL Assessment; orig. pub. King's College).

Bloom, B. S. (1956). *Taxonomy of Educational Objectives. Handbook 1: The Cognitive Domain*. New York: David McKay Co. Inc.

Butler, R. (1998). Enhancing and undermining intrinsic motivation, *British Journal of Educational Psychology* 58: 1–14.

Department for Education and Skills (DfES) (2005). *14–19 Education and Skills White Paper*. Available at: <http://webarchive.nationalarchives.gov.uk/20130401151715/https://www.education.gov.uk/publications/standard/publicationdetail/page1/Cm%206476>

Didau, D. (2013). Work scrutiny: what's the point of marking books?, *The Learning Spy* (26 January). Available at: <http://www.learningspy.co.uk/assessment/work-scrutiny-whats-the-point-of-marking-books/#more-2495>

Didau, D. (2013). Marking is an act of love, *The Learning Spy* (6 October). Available at: <http://www.learningspy.co.uk/assessment/marking-act-love/>

Dweck, C. (2006). *Mindset: The New Psychology of Success*. New York: Ballantine Books.

Excellence Gateway Treasury (n.d.). Effective teaching and learning: effective questioning toolkit. Available at: <http://tlp.excellencegateway.org.uk/tlp/pedagogy/tools/effectivequesti2/index.html>

Forster, F., Hounsell, D. and Thompson, S. (1995). *Tutoring and Demonstrating: A Handbook*. Edinburgh and Sheffield: University of Edinburgh, Centre for Teaching, Learning and Assessment and Committee of Vice-Chancellors and Principals, Universities' and Colleges' Staff Development Agency.

Foster, A. (2005). *Realising the Potential: A Review of the Future Role of Further Education Colleges* [Foster Review]. Department for Education and Skills: Annesley. Available at: <http://repository.excellencegateway.org.uk/fedora/objects/import-pdf:17490/datastreams/PDF/content>

Gadsby, C. (2012). *Perfect Assessment for Learning*. Carmarthen: Independent Thinking Press.

Hattie, J. (2009). *Visible Learning: A Synthesis of Over 800 Meta-Analyses Relating to Achievement*. Abingdon and New York: Routledge.

Hattie, J. (2012). *Visible Learning for Teachers: Maximising Impact on Learning*. London and New York: Routledge.

Holt, J. (1964). *How Children Fail*. New York: Pitman.

Kounin, J. S. (1977). *Discipline and Group Management in Classrooms*. Huntington, NY: R. E. Krieger.

Learning and Skills Improvement Service (2009). *Move On to World Class Skills. Delivering the Goods: Supporting Staff in Logistics to Improve Their English and Maths*. Milton Keynes and Taunton: Move On and Skills for Logistics. Available at: <http://www.moveon.org.uk/downloadsFile/downloads2942/Skills_for_Logistics_toolkit_Jun09_v2.pdf>

McVey, D. (2013). Learn smarter with technology in the classroom, *FE News* (23 August). Available at: <http://www.fenews.co.uk/fe-news/learn-smarter-with-technology-in-the-classroom>

Nash, I., Jones, S., Ecclestone, K. and Brow, A. (2008). *Challenge and Change in Further Education: A Commentary by the Teaching and Learning Research Programme*. London: Teaching and Learning Research Programme and Economic and Social Research Council. Available at: <http://www.tlrp.org/pub/documents/FEcommentary.pdf>

Ofsted (2012a). *Common Inspection Framework for Further Education and Skills 2012*. Ref: 120062. Available at: <http://www.ofsted.gov.uk/resources/common-inspection-framework-for-further-education-and-skills-2012>

Ofsted (2012b). *The Report of her Majesty's Chief Inspector of Education, Children's Services and Skills: Learning and Skills*. Ref: 120350. Available at: <http://www.ofsted.gov.uk/resources/120350>

Ofsted (2013a). *Swindon College: Learning and Skills Inspection Report* (5 April). Available at: <http://www.ofsted.gov.uk/inspection-reports/find-inspection-report/provider/ELS/130849>

Ofsted (2013b). *Walsall College: Learning and Skills Inspection Report* (20 March). Available at: <http://www.ofsted.gov.uk/inspection-reports/find-inspection-report/provider/ELS/130483>

Ofsted (2013c). *Working Men's College: Learning and Skills Inspection Report* (30 April). Available at: <http://www.ofsted.gov.uk/inspection-reports/find-inspection-report/provider/ELS/130403>

Ofsted (2014). *Handbook for the Inspection of Further Education and Skills*. Ref: 120061. Available at: <http://www.ofsted.gov.uk/resources/handbook-for-inspection-of-further-education-and-skills-september-2012>

Petty, G. (2009). *Evidence-Based Teaching: A Practical Approach*, 2nd edn. Cheltenham: Nelson Thornes.

Qualifications and Curriculum Authority (QCA) (2008). *QCA Guidelines on Recording Personal, Learning and Thinking Skills in the Diploma*. Available at: <http://dera.ioe.ac.uk/9322/1/QCAGuidelinesRecordingPLTSiDiploma.pdf>

Reed, J. and Stoltz, P. G. (2011). *Put Your Mindset to Work*. London: Penguin.

Toffler. A. (1973). *Future Shock*. London: Pan Books.

Tuckman, B. (1965). Developmental sequence in small groups, *Psychological Bulletin* 63(6): 384–399.

Wiliam, D. (2007). Content then process: teacher learning communities in the service of formative assessment. In D. B. Reeves (ed.), *Ahead of the Curve: The Power of Assessment to Transform Teaching and Learning*. Bloomington, IN: Solution Tree Press, pp. 183–204.

Wiliam, D. (2011). *Embedded Formative Assessment*: Bloomington, IN: Solution Tree Press.